Decorating
Your Garden

Decorating
Your Garden

Text by Jeff Cox

Photographs by
Jerry Pavia

Abbeville Press Publishers

New York   London   Paris

 # Contents

Introduction

Nature is so full of purposes that her wild landscapes confuse us. There's much more information in the wilderness than we can comprehend. The closer we look, the more we see, until it all shimmers out into visual white noise, beyond our sensory grasp or our intellectual capacity to understand.

In the grand ecology of the wild, nature has plenty of uses for the dead tree limbs that litter the forest floor in a tangled jumble. But when we garden, we simplify. We clear away the detritus of life. Like a sculptor revealing the statue hidden in the stone, we remove things until the picture freshens for us, and becomes more comprehensible. Through simplification we make a defined bit of nature—the garden—understandable, and through decoration we make it appealing to our senses.

Our gardens begin with simple ideas: making a woodland path through the property, or a bed of perennials for color all season long. Nature, on the other hand, embroiders a million ideas into every bit of her natural scenery: A root exudes a substance on which a fungus will feed; the fungus takes phosphorus from the surrounding soil and feeds it back to the plant; the plant provides food for the larvae of the armyworm; and adult armyworms feed the wrens. The cycle spirals onward through the web of life, until we come, by a commodious and nearly infinite recirculation, back to the root we started with.

In the garden, we arrange plants in ways that reflect our human essence, whereas nature provides for the needs of all the creatures present. We repeat groups of the same plant at regular intervals—a form of regularity seldom, if ever, found in the wild. We place plants in sites where they wouldn't naturally occur. And we import plants from around the world to grow side by side with natives. Modern gardens are very much like modern cities—melting pots of individuals from just about everywhere.

Although we may design our gardens and place plants as we will, we cannot exclude wild nature. All the energies, tendencies, and habits that characterize a plant in its native home are still part of its genetic code. As every gardener soon discovers, plants react to nature's imperatives before they do our bidding.

A garden, then, is a mixture of human intention and the plants' obedience to their innate drives, whose purposes are hidden from human view. We may believe

Above: *Does the water-smoothed stone decorate the plants, or vice versa? Grassy sprays of blue-green* Helictotrichon sempervirens *burst from behind the stone set into a flagstone patio, overtopped with sunny bunches of* Oenothera berlandieri *in Barbara Poole's garden in Portola Valley, California.*

Page 6: *Nature is simplified to a salient Japanese maple, then decorated with wooden pilings to hold the pond's bank at David Hungerford's garden in Hunt Valley, Maryland. The scene is so charming that Nature reflects on it in her watery mirror, approving it by improving it.*

we are in control of the garden—we choose and place our plants; we uproot them, divide them, and move, prune, pinch, and thin them. But part of the delight of gardening surely comes from nature laughing at our pomposity. Our control is mostly illusory.

Plants continue to react as always, with a relentless dedication to their inner truths, quickly reestablishing themselves after our intervention, the ultimate arbiters of their own fates. They display their limbs and leaves in ways they deem appropriate. They twist and turn to maximize the light their leaves receive. They shy away and die away from soil they don't like, or light that is too bright or too dark.

The choicest beauties of the garden are usually unplanned. I've seen a lady banks rose climb up through an apple tree, sending down showers of little pastel yellow flowers amid the tree's upwelling pink-and-white blossoms. The casual encounter of rose and tree is given a twist, and we suddenly perceive such great beauty that we fall silent. Now the unspoken message of the one who controls chance can reach our hearts: I am here. I am not far away. You are all mine—you, the tree, and the rose.

The soil is the part of the garden from which everything arises. It is the mother of us all, into which the spirit blows life, and out of which come peonies and people. The soil is the source and destiny of all life. Plants spring from it and die back into it yearly. It takes us longer, but so do we. Soil is the archive of all past seasons and the raw material of the future. Our part is to care for it, improve it, and add to its richness.

Finally, the garden has an aspect that is purely human. This part includes the fences, walkways, patios, terraces, arbors, pergolas, gazebos, walls, hutches, skeps, birdhouses, waterfalls, pools, tables, chairs, benches, lighting, and bridges. Here we can also include constructs made from soil, rocks, and water: berms, pits, hollows, grottoes, leveled places, and peaks of the landscape's architecture. In other words, it's everything in the garden but the plants.

Here wild nature pretty much gives way to our human desires. Here we are finally in charge, with the power to do what we wish with the land. This power brings responsibility, however. We must remember that we don't see all of nature's purposes, or fully understand her motives. We should create our gardens humbly, and decorate them with as much taste as we can muster.

Part of the great, grand fun of creating a garden is to infuse it with personal meaning, or with purely human ideas that visitors can comprehend.

Take as an example my clamshell garden. I grew up near the shores of the Atlantic Ocean, and digging in the soil of my backyard, I often unearthed clamshells deposited there thousands of years before, when our property was shoreline. Today, I have a small side garden where I have buried many clamshells left over from the times when they were part of our nightly dinners, months or even years ago. Now when I dig there to put in annuals or divide perennials, I usually unearth a shell or two, and I am pleasantly transported back to my early childhood on Long Island.

My clamshells are personal; but everyone can relate to another of my favorite garden devices: a place of refuge-and-vista. The refuge may be a bench placed back in the shadows of a leafy bower, and the vista, seen from the bench, is of a sunny, open space where one can secretly watch the world go by. This kind of idea appeals to nearly all visitors.

Personal and human expression determines how we decorate our gardens. This book is devoted to describing the many ways people decorate their gardens, and the many things they use in this pursuit. The purpose of decorating a garden—which we often (incorrectly) assume is decorative enough with no help from us—is not to gild the lily, but to enshrine the lily in a place that illuminates its transcendent beauty.

—Jeff Cox

Big-leaved bergenia (Bergenia cordifolia) *in the foreground and blue-violet* Campanula portenschlagiana *farther down the brick path lead one to the rose-covered arbor that marks the transition from garden to lawn beyond. This is Cynthia Woodyard's garden in Portland, Oregon. Such places of contrasting terrain call for a dramatic effect, like the arbor.*

CHAPTER ONE

Landscaping and Hardscaping the Terrain

 ## The Garden Begins in a Dream

We fantasize about a special place in nature, one of loveliness and succor. When we dwell on it, we begin to build a picture in our imaginations of just how this garden should look, with all the features we hold most dear, and all the things we find most appealing. At this point, the garden is made of gossamer imagination—airy stuff, easily changed, torn down, or built up to suit our whims. There is a reality to these dreams, for they embody what we love. They are at the core, and they precede action. As Shakespeare said, "We are such stuff as dreams are made on, and our little life is rounded with a sleep" (*The Tempest*, 4.1).

The word *garden* is both verb and noun. As verb, it encompasses the work of expressing our intent, setting our dreams to action. As a noun, it defines the finished product—although true gardeners find that their gardens are never completed for more than a moment, until a new idea takes shape and is carried out. As long as dreams come spinning up out of our hearts, our gardens are ever in the process of becoming.

Our gardens come to embody what we love—not only the plants that are our familiar and dear friends, but also the garden's structure, which allows us those comforts for which we garden in the first place. The landscape of the garden is the landscape of our dreams—or at least it should be. First, however, we must have vivid dreams, the better to bring

them to life. Blurred images and shifting plans make for gardens that slide into incomprehensibility.

The process of landscaping a piece of property such as a yard begins with some daydreaming. I have done this daydreaming two ways, both of which seem to work.

In the first way, I simply make myself comfortable, close my eyes, and summon pleasant memories. I don't care whether they are memories of childhood, of youth, or adulthood—although I find that most often, I am back in my early youth. Childhood memories have mythic qualities, since they are the kernels around which our view of the world crystallizes.

One such dream session carried me back to a time when I was four or five years old. Our family—my mom and dad, my older sister and brother, and myself—lived

on Long Island in a place called Norgate, a pleasant development of nice homes built in the 1930s. At the two entrances to Norgate stood square brick pillars, painted white with black tops, on which were large, round, white glass globes that glowed softly in the evening. At the northern end of the development, the pillar was planted with shrubbery. I remember two hydrangea bushes under which I used to hide, waiting for my father to come home on the commuter train from Manhattan.

From the rail stop he walked through a parking lot, around a large elementary school, and through the playground; then he crossed the street to enter Norgate by the pillar. I'd hide patiently in the bushes until I could see him coming across the playground, briefcase in hand, fedora on his head. When he was a little way past the pillar, I'd come out silently and run to him from behind, jumping up on his back to surprise him.

He, of course, never failed to be completely surprised when I jumped up and hugged him, even though I repeated this ritual every day when the weather was clement. He'd laugh and kiss me, then swing me up on his shoulders to ride in triumph for the two-block walk home.

There is now a place in a garden that I created where a path meanders past a white-and-black brick pillar topped with a round globe light. The pillar is surrounded by hydrangea bushes.

As I contemplated the finished work, I was carried back to Norgate, and could see in my mind's eye the old playground across the street. And then I could see my father's ghost come walking toward the pillar, a tall and slender man with a purposeful gait coming home once again, and my young spirit—still alive somewhere within me—rushed to greet him. It is not a memorable spot, perhaps, for

Opposite: Carefully arranged stones in front of this ocean-viewing platform give some bulk and substance to a seaside landscape that would otherwise be featureless. Yet the designer hasn't made the mistake of making a structure so high it interferes with the breathtaking sweep of sand and sea in front of the viewer.

Page 10: The sweep of light stones creates a river-like effect through the low part of the Stein family's garden, designed by Shirley Kerins, in Pasadena, California, bringing movement and the suggestion of water to a dry landscape. The bright stream of rocks is emphasized by the light foliage of Festuca *'Bluefinch' and* Artemisia *'Powis Castle', which carry the eye to the background, while dark green shrubs on the left and a sea of rich pink verbena on the right define this stream's "banks."*

anyone but me—but so what? Our gardens should be full of such associations, formed from memories and dreams, able to touch us deeply and secretly.

Another time, I daydreamed about a warm afternoon in Quebec City. I was in my early twenties, and was visiting Quebec with a college friend on Labor Day weekend. We'd met a couple of young French Canadian women at lunch, and afterward walked to the historic Citadelle at the edge of the Plains of Abraham, where Wolfe defeated Montcalm high on the cliffs above the wide Saint Lawrence River. We lay on a grassy bank, and the view was tremendous: below us were the fairy-tale towers of the Château Frontenac, and the Saint Lawrence, criss-crossed by the ferry to Levis, sweeping away in a huge vista to the east and the sea. The sun and the company were warm, and above

us, fighter jets roared by, issuing red, white, and blue smoke in honor of the American holiday.

It was an unforgettable moment of pure pleasure. The site was fairly easy to suggest in a garden by making a berm that faced south to catch the sun, with a view across the yard planted with a sweeping river of grass. Most of the berm was given over to shrubs and flowering plants, but a central portion was planted with grass that flowed down to meet the lawn. After a long, cold winter, that grassy bank became a prime area for early May sunbathing, re-creating some of the warmth I experienced on that bank in Canada, high above the Saint Lawrence, 35 years ago.

The second way of daydreaming involves superimposing dreams on an existing piece of property. One can do this by simply sitting down at the site and imagining what might become of the place you're looking at, but I find that a flat, horizontal view across a property is not a very rewarding way to look at it. If possible, look down on the place where the garden will go. If a house or structure is nearby, go to an upstairs window or up on the roof. If no structure is nearby, climb a tree if you can. Even climbing to the top of a stepladder will give you some height, and the added inspiration and ideas that go with a changed point of view.

I used this technique when I moved to a new house that had an unattractive and overgrown border of shrubs and trees out front. I filled a glass with ice and lemonade, went to an upstairs window that overlooked the border, and removed the

window screen. Then I spent a good long time at the window, looking at the overgrown border, contemplatively sipping my lemonade, and daydreaming.

At first I noticed that there was a tree definitely worth keeping—an old, gnarly boled apple tree with plenty of character. Scrubby shrubbery around it was removed in a second by my imagination, and I soon knew what I would keep, what I would remove, and what I would cut back.

Looking down, I noticed that the apple tree's limbs had a natural whorl to them as they emerged from the trunk, and I thought that their whirling pattern might be reflected by paving on the ground. Brick is a good natural color, so I imagined a set of three broad steps that rose the 2 feet from the level of the lawn to the level of the border. At the top of the steps, I could see that a brick path might swing around the tree and exit farther down the border, and traced its shape with my finger. I could also see that in the space between the trunk and the path, a nice feature such as a small water pond would lend stability to the sweeping path.

After about a half hour or so of such daydreaming, I went down and inspected the border and discovered that all my imaginings might be accomplished without too much trouble. Soon I was bringing my dreams to life. Out came old shrubs, in went the path and the small pond, and when it was done, it all looked fine—but something was missing.

After another session at the upstairs window, I noticed that the newly opened parts of the border, where I planned to put semi-shade perennials and small evergreen shrubs, were shapeless and flat. Something architectural was needed on which to hang the new plantings. I imagined a large group of rocks, somewhat away from the path, to balance the tight

A gravel path and garden are expertly separated by a pretty escarpment of mossy stones. Notice how designer Gordon Hayward, who installed this garden for Barry Waxman in Putney, Vermont, uses the flash of light blue oat grass (Helictotrichon sempervirens) to set off the light-colored rock, while he pairs the dark Japanese barberry (Berberis thunbergii 'Atropurpurea Nana') with the dark rock. Tall green grasses echo the oat grass, while the burgundy flower heads of Sedum 'Autumn Joy' harmonize with the barberry's color.

coil of path and pond. Back outside, I saw that the rocks would indeed balance the composition of the area, giving weight to the opened area away from the tree. I realized then, for the first time, that plants seldom carry the kind of visual weight that rocks and other hardscaping provide. Plants are evanescent creatures—even when they are large evergreens. But rocks are forever.

Within a day, two burly fellows from a local supplier of landscape materials wrestled three huge stones into the shape I had envisioned, and the structure of the garden was complete. Because the landscape was right, plants now became easy to site. They fit into the discrete spaces created by path, pond, tree, and the large, half-buried stones.

Gardens thus can be places where the terrain itself—soil and rocks and water—emerges concretely from the ocean of dreams within us.

Moving Earth for Pleasing and Decorative Effects

◉ Berms

One moves earth only after giving the matter due deliberation. First of all, it's expensive. Second, it can be very messy, with a heavy backhoe or tracked earthmover crossing your yard or breaking up areas of asphalt or concrete. Third, it can be hazardous to buried conduits for water, gas, and electricity, to leach fields and sewage lines, and to existing paths and walkways. Fourth, it can be very disruptive to existing vegetation that you may want to preserve as you rearrange your landscape.

There are many situations, however, when moving earth is called for. Your property may be board flat and uninteresting, for example, or have awkward piles of spoils from cellar excavations or nature's carelessness. Sometimes the lay of the land presents landscape plantings badly, making them slope away from the house, for instance,

when you'd much rather they rise slightly. If the site is sloped to funnel rainwater right into your gardens or into your cellar, you might want to consider moving the earth around.

The simplest way is to bring in several truckloads of soil to make mounds, berms, or banks of soil on which to elevate plantings, beds, and borders.

A *berm* in landscaping is a raised mound of earth, or the shoulder of a slope where a path may run—most often the former. Berms can help define a space,

such as a yard, where the terrain may be fairly level and undefined as it runs off into adjacent properties. They can also be stages for plantings, much as risers are stages for ranks of choristers.

A well-placed berm can also be a decorative element in the landscape. It may curve gently through a space, or along the back of the property, lending a curvaceous element to a rectangular yard. It may also run straight along a boundary or even—if the landscaper feels "creative"—bisect a yard. I have seen one

Nicely graded flat stones make formal terraces in Sharon Abroms's garden in Atlanta. The rockwork terraces elevate the lettuces, basil, peppers, and mustard greens and provide a platform for the pyramidal wooden tomato cages. The design is as much landscape art as it is practical vegetable garden.

space bisected by crossing berms forming an ✕ and creating four discrete hollows in its arms. Although the effect was striking, I'm not sure it was pleasing at all, as it was disruptive, unnatural, and difficult to read as well as negotiate.

For my taste, berms are aptly created and placed when they border a lawn that's to be used by a family for playing on and enjoying the view from, and when they carry a gentle curve that in some way echoes the natural lay of the land, an adjoining street, a curving patio, or other feature.

Gentle is the watchword with a berm. Too high and it may be not only awkward

looking but also unstable in rains, creating its own little California mudslide. Too low and it becomes more of a nuisance than a berm. For most spaces, a berm about 4 or 5 feet tall (1.5 m), either gently rounded over its width or flattened on top, gives a subdued appearance. It should be twice as wide at its base as it is high. Such a soil structure can add a feeling of privacy to a portion of the property, such as a backyard.

Rather than just dumping soil, however, it's a good idea to have the area of

the berm defined by large rocks—the bigger the better, actually. These can then be covered with soil that will wash down between the rocks, which in turn will hold the bank together through heavy rains that may erode unsupported soil.

As soon as the berm is constructed, cover it with grass seed or thick mulch. The grass roots will help stabilize the soil during rains when it is still loose and relatively uncompacted. Mulch will absorb the pounding effect of raindrops, allowing

the water to trickle through to soil level, where it will be less likely to erode the newly moved earth.

After construction, you can put in other elements, such as stones, statuary, herbaceous perennials, and woody plants, by removing turves from the berm, or

Above: Mr. and Mrs. Charles Stein solved the problem of how to handle a steep hillside by their Pasadena, California, home with a decorative yet simple, easy-to-make, and inexpensive terrace. Railroad ties are cut with a chain saw into steps set this way and that for interest, while preservative-treated logs are held in place by metal bars.

Opposite: An awkward bank becomes a gorgeous rock garden at the Vancouver home of the Peck family. Dianthus, campanulas, and geraniums—among other perennials—are interspersed with imported stones to bring this site to vibrant life.

pulling aside the mulch. If you plant grass, do so on a south-facing area, where you'll be able to relax and feel the returning sun's warmth in the early spring. You probably don't want to have to mow the whole berm, but I have seen all-grass berms that give a very decorative look to a property.

Another decorative idea is a series of berms, with a low one at the front, followed by a medium one, with a rather taller one in back—like a series of waves rolling in from the ocean, or like sand dunes on a beach echoing the waves. If you use repeating berms, they will probably be covered with grass or groundcovers, because large woody plants grown on such repeating berms would soon overgrow them and hide their pleasing shape. Thus you might want to scale down this idea, because the grass or groundcover

will need mowing or maintenance, and you don't want to make more work for yourself than is necessary.

A berm is not only decorative itself, but also an ideal spot for decoration. The rise of earth and vegetation behind ornamental stones, statuary, or furniture gives them a secure look, anchoring them to the garden. Garden accoutrements that are sitting on flat ground, or on terrain that is sloping away from the viewer, visually seem more ready to float off.

Berms also function to separate areas of the landscape. A driveway, for instance, is often difficult to integrate into a well-designed garden. Why not use a berm to separate the driveway area from the garden proper? A pathway through the berm, with an arched arbor supporting a vine, makes the transition from driveway to garden well-defined and pleasing (see page 169).

◉ Banks

Banks work best on steadily sloping property, because such terrain can make you feel woozy if you spend much time there. I once owned a house on an acre with a steady 15-degree slope. After living there for a short time, I realized that every view of the terrain from every window was of a tilted plane, even though the trees, of course, grew to a true vertical. I knew that a flat, level place was needed so I could orient and anchor myself to the earth.

Right in front of the house, I excavated the soil to about 3 feet (1 m) deep. The excavated soil was pushed out flat to fill a large area, a process that created two banks. The upper bank was the original

bank, with a water feature to remind me of true level.

Steep banks offer a challenge to the gardener. Covered with grass, they are hard to mow. Terracing is a great idea and will result in level areas for planting, but terraces take considerable work to establish. A good way to handle a bank is to put in permanent plants—evergreens of all kinds, small or low-growing deciduous woody shrubs, larger deciduous shrubs, even ornamental trees, whose roots will hold the bank when rains come. But banks also offer a pleasing slope for decorative work such as I'll discuss throughout this book, including solutions like waterfalls, stone assemblages, sculpture, and cleverly constructed steps.

A bank may also serve as a slope joining two levels of the landscape—an arrangement that allows the installation of steps, arches over the steps, and the possibility of turning the bank into a stone or brick wall, with the upper and lower levels both flat and leveled, so that you maximize the amount of level space. To create this look, level the upper half (or

portion) of a gently sloping piece of property. Move the excavated soil to the lower half, leveling it there, also. The banked slope between the two levels can either be planted or cut perpendicularly and faced with a wall.

The top of a bank is an interesting place to put a walkway, especially if it allows you to look down on plantings below. If a naturally occurring stream or watercourse lies at the bottom of the bank, so much the better, but even dry land offers a gardener a place to install decorative elements that can be seen from above. As with dreaming about your property's potential, the view from above is different and unusual. Take advantage of such a view if you have it.

A vista I once encountered in Italy is a good example. I was following a pathway alongside a winery when I saw a fine use of a bank as a vantage point. On my left was the wall of the winery, richly patinated with age and covered with a climbing vine—parthenocissus, I believe. On my right, a bank, with large rock outcroppings interplanted with evergreens, plummeted to a flat area below, where artisans had laid out a patio constructed of several types and colors of stone. It wasn't a mosaic so much as a geometric design, and from above, the effect was striking. I think gardeners who already have a bank on their property, or a slope that can be relatively easily cut and filled to make a bank, are lucky, for the terrain then has interest, and the gardener's job is to take advantage of its effect from above and below.

cut, and the second bank was where the fill dropped away to rejoin the sloping terrain. This cut-and-fill operation gave me a rounded, free-form level place about 60 by 80 feet (18 x 24 m) directly in front of the house. At the base of the upper bank I installed a small pool for water lilies. Water, of course, is the master substance when it comes to finding true level. For comparatively small expense, I now had an oasis of flat lawn bordering a raised

◉ Hollows and Channels

An acquaintance of mine bought a 1920s-style bungalow perched atop a steep bank, with concrete steps leading up two landings to the front door. Behind the house was a small backyard and a garage accessible from an alley. It was a boring facade, the same as every other house on his street. One day he said he'd made great changes, and invited me over to his house to see. But he wanted it to be a surprise, and wouldn't tell me what these changes were.

When I arrived, I didn't know the place. He'd hollowed out a broad walkway leading back into the bank, excavating right to the concrete foundation of the house. He'd redone the basement into a finished family room, and punched through the foundation wall to install

....

Opposite: The presence of native stone on a steep bank is used to advantage at Barbara Poole's garden in Portola Valley, California. Steps made of wooden railroad ties have been set into the bank and planted with the tiny white daisies of Erigeron karvinskianus, *purple lobelia, and the grassy blue-green spray of* Helictotrichon sempervirens. *The stones have been used to flank the steps, yet they retain a naturalistic look.*

Right: Water from the Great Lakes deposited minerals on the surface of these stones in the Milwaukee garden of the Black family, giving them varied and interesting patinas. The stones give weight and earthy substance to an ethereal stand of Echinacea pallida, *whose pink prairie coneflowers fly upward like a covey of startled birds. They also hide the spot where the fence post is sunk into the earth. Grouping them in a trio enhances their stability.*

sliding glass doors. Where the foundation walls were now showing, he sealed them against water and gave them a facing of native stone. Now one entered the house through the basement level, rather than going up two flights of ordinary-looking concrete steps outside. He figured it would be better to climb steps inside the house than outside when snow and ice coated everything.

Instead of building straight walls along the sides of the excavation, he'd had large boulders brought in and placed along the sides, cementing them at the bottom into the walkway.

In the center of this walkway he'd installed a huge, beautiful boulder that blocked the view into the family room from the street, and made the entrance more interesting. On top of the boulder banks he planted creeping junipers and other trailers that hung down in festoons over the rock surfaces, softening and brightening them.

The effect was bold, dramatic, and fun. And he'd turned an old basement into a usable room.

The idea is that besides building up soil in berms and banks, one can also create decorative landscape terrain by removing soil and creating hollows and channels back into existing banks. This technique isn't limited to entrances to a house, but can also be used out in a garden, where a path that otherwise would require a climb can be dug out of hilly terrain so that it rises only slightly, if at all, as it winds through a garden with slopes. At some points the path will be at ground level, and at other points it may be below ground level, giving the gardener a chance to show off his or her skill by planting up the banks that are created on each side. The path may sometimes meander over an existing low spot, requiring a bridge—another chance to show off one's skill in helping people to glide through the garden rather than labor up and down steep slopes.

When creating channels and hollows, take a tip from my friend who redid his entrance so cleverly, and place a decorative object—statue, sundial, stone—in the hollow where the eye is drawn. Hollows and channels are natural funnels for the path of the gaze, and if you are going to create something that so strongly pulls the eye, then place something there worth seeing.

Smoothing and Glorifying Rough, Difficult, or Awkward Places

Sometimes nature, or the builders, leaves a property with lumpy mounds of soil, or awkward channels carved out of the earth, that would be much more appealing if smoothed out a bit. Try to visualize whether and how a day's work with a backhoe could improve your property.

The chief purpose of smoothing a rough landscape is to bring grace to an awkward contour. Gracefulness is in the eye of the beholder, I suppose, but I find gentle slopes more graceful and relaxing than steep ones; gently sweeping, round corners more graceful than sharp, boxy ones; and horizontal lines more restful and graceful than vertical ones. Give your property the once-over. It may need no smoothing, but then again, you may discover a spot that interrupts a graceful line and decide to do something with it.

Remember that on property that hasn't been worked over, nature has devised strict ways for excess rainwater to run off. Whenever you change the lay of the land, you change the way water will run off. Always bring your low point either to a place where you would want water to collect or drain away, or to the place where rainwater already naturally drains away. Avoid creating low cul-de-sacs where water can accumulate. The best way to avoid drainage problems when smoothing a landscape is to follow nature's original contours, but simply smooth them out.

Stone as a Decorative Element in the Landscape

Working with Naturally Occurring Rock

I count those gardeners most fortunate who have natural rock outcroppings, or even large, loose stones on their properties. As with established trees, my rule for rocks is, unless they are disruptive and ugly, leave them as they are, using them as the basis for your garden planning.

If your property already has stones in it, then the stones are native by definition,

are color coordinated (unless it's one of those rare boulder fields of different rocks brought together by glacial action), and have a coherent look and similar texture.

At the upper edge of some property I once owned, on a wooded hillside, were huge, glacier-ground boulders; the smallest was the size of an automobile, and the largest the size of a house. They had been deposited there when glaciers melted, about 17,000 years before, and had settled into a sturdy pile with space between the boulders for climbing through. This rock formation was so dramatic that it affected how one thought of the property, and when my wife and I created a garden down on more level land out in the sun, we chose as the central focus a very large rock similar to those in the woods. Over this rock we built a rustic arbor with four posts. One post supported a red 'Don Juan' rose, another carried a white-flowered sweet autumn clematis, the third a blue wisteria, and the fourth a

A tide of light pink thyme washes over and around beautiful boulders used to anchor the Roberts family garden in Friday Harbor, Washington. The busy little leaves and flowers of the plants contrast nicely with the big homogeneous bulk of the stones. Imagine how weak this garden would look without the stones.

yellow honeysuckle. Each vine was fragrant, and each had a different season of bloom and showed a different flower color; there was always something adding

Left: *Stone is the feature in the Berg family's New Hampshire garden. Dan Snow used cut stones for formality, dressed stone to make tightly knit walls, and passages of natural cobbles to give some spontaneity to the design. A water trough and flume arrangement brings the movement of water to the design. Plants here are an afterthought.*

Below: *In another part of the Bergs' garden, Dan Snow used monumental boulders in a naturalistic arrangement, then connected them with interlocking walls of dressed stones. The stonework is strongly dominant, and only partially softened and integrated by the oak tree, flowering sedum, and tall miscanthus grass atop the terrace.*

color and perfuming the air. This arrangement was a bit of homage to the central stone, which we thought of as representative of the immense and beautiful stones hidden in the forest above.

At another spot on the property, we found a bank covered with rough weeds, like greenbrier, sumac, poison ivy, and bindweed, as well as some not-so-rough native herbaceous perennials such as *Smilacina racemosa*. One of our first jobs was to dig out the rough stuff, and as the work progressed, we found that ages of

decaying plants had created topsoil that covered very large boulders.

For weeks we dug out buckets and buckets of small stones and soil full of weed roots from atop and between the stones. Slowly they revealed themselves as beautiful sandstone boulders that eventually bleached in the sun to a lovely light yellow-ocher. We left their back ends buried in the bank and excavated their faces down to the level of the lawn that they abutted. I used the largest native stones we'd removed to make a 20-foot

Inspiration abounds in this herb and perennial garden at John and Daphne Chappell's Cinerdine Cottage in Gloucestershire, England. Dressed stone and pavers edge a sunken ring of gravel, where lavender, euphorbia, thyme, and dianthus dance. The gravel allows rainwater to drain straight down, where it then flows away.

(6.1 m) dry stone wall that swung out gently from one of the big rocks, then returned to meet the last of the big rocks at the end of the bank. It formed a terrace

23

Japanese gardens are subtle evocations of nature glorified, and require exquisite human taste to achieve. This fine example in the Portland Japanese Garden, Portland, Oregon, has a traditional arrangement of stone watercourse, waterfall, and pond. The single stone in the pond harmonizes with the shape and thrust of the stones behind it. Note that the vegetation is wood and foliage—no flowers—a typically Japanese garden idea.

about 2½ feet high and about 3 feet wide (76 x 91 cm). I then filled it with topsoil and planted it with choice little perennials like dianthus 'Tiny Rubies', *Armeria maritima*, geranium 'Ingwerson's Variety', and other favorites that would remain well behaved in their bed atop the stone wall. Between two of the largest boulders I built a set of steps that brought people up to the vegetable gardens, vineyard, and fruit orchard. Along these steps I planted *Aubrieta deltoides, Iberis sempervirens,*

Alyssum saxatile, and other busy little plants perfect for the site.

This place was a prime example of someone's good fortune—mine! Here was property as stony as a Puritan preacher. It became a showplace primarily because of the imposing boulders that we either glorified or revealed. I encourage you to check your place for any rock outcroppings or individual large boulders that can be excavated or revealed, and used as the focus for an entire garden.

◉ Stones as the Bones of an Ornamental Garden

Just as a skeleton gives shape to animal flesh, so stones give shape to the ornamental garden. It is possible to make a fine garden without stone, but stones are enormously important to achieve the following results, which are closely related:

• To create discrete planting areas. Without stone, how else are you going to easily and dramatically separate one area of green, growing plants from another? By interposing stone between planting areas, you visually punctuate the garden so that—to use a writer's metaphor—the areas may be read as different paragraphs, rather than the garden as one long, confusing run-on sentence.

• To alleviate endless amounts of green and provide essential contrast with plant life. Most of the garden is green for most of the season, with lots and lots of busy leaves. Large areas of dark, smooth stone give relief from all that green. Areas of living green plants acquire enhanced grandeur and meaning when contrasted with inanimate objects like large stones.

• To suggest the monumental forces lying beneath the soil. These forces find expression in stones that project above the soil surface and interrupt and add interest to otherwise plain expanses of flat land. We don't often think about it, but beneath the soil surface, the processes of mountain building, erosion, subsidence, folding, heaving, and melting are continuous; swirling rivers of white-hot magma creep and flow. The stones that reach the surface are less than the tip of the iceberg. In rare instances, we can see the evidence of these massive geological forces, in dramatic landscapes like the Delaware Water Gap, where layers upon layers of stone have been heaved nearly vertical. These are the pages of Earth's history book—the Jurassic and Triassic layers, the Devonian, on back to, finally, the Pre-Cambrian rocks that predate life on the planet.

◉ Siting and Installing Stone

On properties that have little in the way of large landscaping stone already in place, you may have to bring some in, or relocate existing stones.

There are some rules for doing this. Placing stones here and there in pretty patterns or placing them next to one another as edging is certainly one way to site stones, and it has a simple decorative appeal. But for an artful landscape, we need a better approach.

Stand on your property and try to imagine the powerful forces that shifted the earth and heaved the rocks to where they are. Imagine those forces flowing through the existing surface and rocks. Augment those force lines with any rocks

A group of stones is heaped up in a naturalistic way to alleviate a flat and uninteresting piece of landscape at Barnsley Gardens in Adairsville, Georgia, then sparsely planted with Scotch broom (Cytisus). Notice that the stones are all of one kind, which helps to visually pull the rockwork together.

An otherwise boring expanse of flagstone terracing is made extraordinarily interesting by a sweet little garden created from a round, warmly colored boulder and the soft, fresh stalks of Santolina chamaecyparissus, *each just beginning to open a yellow flower head. Succulents and evergreens spill onto the terrace beneath the rock in this private garden in Montecito, California.*

you bring in, so that, like the bones of the body, they fit into the direction of those forces in commonsensical ways that look and feel right.

If your property is just flat soil, as on the prairie, look at the horizon for evidence of geological forces. Imagine what would happen if the continental shield burst open and heaved up stones right through your property! Good stone placement can suggest a huge, unified force bursting through, giving all the stones a shove in the same direction, and perhaps allowing some to push all the way out of the ground and tumble back over others coming up from beneath.

This is just one way to visualize stone placement.

If you visit a Japanese or Chinese garden, you'll see that stone placement has been raised to a fine art. It is not simply nature that sites stones, but a human mind that respects nature and pays artistic homage to her—but remains human nevertheless. A well-made Japanese garden is like a poem. One definition of a poem is writing where each word is essential, and where any change would destroy the whole. Like words in a poem, each rock in the Japanese garden is placed in the perfect position relative to all the others, and to the water and plantings.

Any change disrupts the poetry of the piece. The arrangement of stones looks natural but refined; a perfect collaboration of artistic sensibility with the forces of nature.

When siting stones artistically, as in the manner of a Japanese garden, look to nature for inspiration. Drive in the countryside and sketch the natural arrangements of stones of whatever size that look most pleasing to you. Take those sketches home and place your stones—of whatever size you have—in similar patterns and arrangements. Look at books of fine

nature photographs or landscape paintings. The stones in those images were chosen by the photographer or painter for their pleasing arrangement. Use the formal artistic elements of balance, weight,

....

Stones of varying size half buried in sand give a very natural look to a river of stones that courses through a garden of succulents and sword-leaved phormiums in San Marcos, California. The river of stones has a practical purpose as well as a decorative one. The stones slow the movement of water from torrential winter rains that would erode unprotected soil.

form, line, and color to site stones well. When you have it right, not a stone will be able to be moved without disturbing the harmony of the piece.

When you have decided on a site, then orienting the stones becomes important. Stones seldom look their best when they are simply sitting atop the ground as if someone had just tossed them there. They are tied to the earth and the garden when they are partially buried. Turn your stones so the heaviest portion is down, and bury some at least one-third, and some two-thirds, into the ground; bury others almost to their tops. Perhaps a stone or two can sit atop the soil, but at least snuggle its bottom into the earth so it doesn't look freshly placed.

Stones that are turned end up and thus project up from the soil really need to be buried at least halfway, or they seem top-heavy and ready to fall. Vary your placement so you have some low, chunky stones and some upended ones poking up from the soil, and arrange the varied shapes in pleasing combinations.

It's ideal to work with just one kind of stone. A piece of broken blue shale among water-smoothed beige sandstone looks out of place. If you use stone from a single locale, the single color, relational form, and qualities of fracture and so forth will help unify the picture. If your stones come from close to home, they will look most natural.

Every arrangement of stone, whether large or small, needs three or more massive stones to give it substance. Lots of little stones look as though they have been dumped from a wheelbarrow. Use smaller stones in and around the big ones. When you put in large stones, think about using some large woody plants to balance and augment them. A large stone paired with a dark green *Chamaecyparis* is a classic combination in any garden.

When siting stones on a gently sloping piece of land, you might want to use them in undulating lines that can allow you to terrace the slope. Several flat pools of garden soil separated from other levels by well-sited rocks give you discrete garden areas in which to try different groups of plants.

▣ Stones as Art

Individual stones of great beauty have been used like sculpture in gardens for centuries. The Chinese are masters of this art form. In fact, some Chinese gardens are entirely made of such stones, with little or no vegetation.

In ancient China, stones were venerated, given names, and were, under the animistic beliefs of old, thought to be endowed with spiritual force. Among the choicest stones were pieces of limestone from the depths of Lake Tai, known as *taihu* stones. In the Forbidden City and the old imperial palaces, among other places, taihu stones were set on pedestals for the enjoyment of the elite. Now everyone can enjoy them, and the Chinese appreciation of this form of beauty is not diminished by its availability.

Taihu stones have a sculptural quality. The moving waters of the lake have worn pockets and indentations in the stones, so they are a riddled mass of undulations. The Chinese think of the convex surfaces as yang, or male energy, and the concave surfaces as yin, or female energy. Taihu stones are objects of contemplation as well as natural sculptures of great beauty.

The Chinese also love miniature stone sculptures. *Penjing*, the Chinese art of miniature gardening from which the Japanese adapted bonsai, usually includes a small water-sculpted stone along with a dwarfed plant in the small flat pot.

In Western gardens, beautiful stones are too seldom given a place of honor. Such stones can be placed at focal points at the end of pathways, down narrow vistas, at the place where two oblique lines meet, by a gate, across water, or anywhere else in the landscape where the eye is drawn. In our tradition, such places are usually given to specimen plants. We also need to think of specimen stones.

Featuring stones as art also calls attention to them, and visitors will want to examine them more closely. The tactile qualities of stone are sensual, and people will naturally run their hands over a featured stone to see what it feels like. Providing such experiences in a garden adds variety and interest.

....

One of the chief functions of a patio is to provide a level space for tables and chairs, as here at the Sacco garden in Tucson. A good, solid surface, rather than soft earth or lawn, keeps furniture from sinking in and tilting. This desert patio features the round Echinocactus grusonii, *plus verbena, agave, and the upright, leafless stalks of ocotillo.*

◉ The River-of-Stones Effect

Most fast-moving rivers throw out areas of stones differentiated by size. Banks of sand, pebbles, cobbles, and larger stones tend to be grouped when fast-moving water tosses and deposits them along the watercourse; sand is carried farthest out from the main channel, and larger stones stay closer.

We can use this knowledge to create the look of a river or stream, even when we don't have water flowing through our gardens (see page 170). By putting a river of stones in our garden landscape, we can re-create the feel of moving water, and by decorating this river with the kind of plants one finds along a riverbank, we can further strengthen the illusion.

When it rains heavily, of course, a well-sited "river" may not be so illusory. The next time it rains hard, take note of the way water runs off your land. If there's an obvious channel or low spot that carries water, then that's a good indication of where a river of stones should go. The stones will allow excess rainwater to flow freely down the course, and the stones will disrupt and slow the fast-flowing water, preventing erosion and damage to the property.

The river of stones is also a fine place for some garden statuary of the type you might find at a real pond or waterway—such as a slinking cat, a heron, or an animal bent to drink.

The river of stones solves several problems at once. It carries away water and prevents erosion. It's a weed-free, relatively low-maintenance area—stones require no care. It gives you a feature to contrast with all that green shrubbery in the garden. It adds grace and beauty as it sweeps through the property. And you may find that bridges built over the river of stones are just as effective decorations

for the garden as bridges over water. Site the bridges where the paths in the garden would naturally cross the "river."

Finally, the river of stones changes in every season, just as a real river does. In the spring and summer it can be floriferous or architectural, as you wish, and in the fall, leaves will blow in to lodge among the rocks. In the winter, it will fill with snow, and at times the rocks will be capped with white hemispheres of snow and ice.

Making Garden Terrain Friendly to Humans

People of all cultures respond to a certain proportion in things. There are absolute proportions that please just about everyone, except for the cantankerous oddballs among us. The "golden section" is one such proportion, and although identified by the ancient Greeks, it is found in architecture in many places around the world.

The use of such proportions in the landscape helps make that landscape satisfying. We feel comfortable in it. The sight of it pleases us and feels right. Some rules of proportion that work for me are:

• Steps should be at least four times wider than their rise—and look even better when the width is more generous.

• Terraces look best when their horizontal beds are about twice as wide as their vertical faces. If you have a terrace with 6-foot (2.36 m) walls holding 3-foot

(1.18 m) beds, it looks awkward. Consider leveling the steep bank.

• By all means, use the golden section when constructing things in the garden. The golden section provides that the ratio of the shorter segment of any line to the larger segment is the same as the larger segment of any line to the whole. Numerically, that's a point .618 units along the entire length (which is always measured as 1.0). Thus, if you are constructing an arbor whose height is 8 feet (2.44 m), then the width would be 4.94 feet (1.51 m) using the golden section. (If 8 is the longer part of the whole, then 4.94 is the shorter part [8 x .618 = 4.94].)

There's another aspect of human-friendliness that has to do with inviting us to walk into a space or negotiate a set of steps. A wide path is more pleasing than a narrow one. A gentle rise on a set of steps is more pleasing than a steep rise. Some say the ideal rise for a step is 6 to 8 inches (15–20 cm), but sometimes steep slopes or rises will require steps with higher risers. At that point, consider whether leveling a steep bank by importing rock and soil might not be a more aesthetic solution than a set of very steep steps. (It certainly will be a more expensive one.) Of course, you can tame a steep rise by having your steps do switchbacks. Steps going straight up a hill are steepest. Going back and forth across the face of the hill allows a much gentler rise—and has the advantage of making the path longer and giving the gardener more opportunity for plantings on the way up.

Having a level place to sit and enjoy the outdoors is also very pleasing. Ever try sleeping on a tilted surface? Not fun at all. Similarly, having a place to root yourself on a level surface gives you an anchored perspective on the grounds, and a place that functions as an outdoor room. The place can be grass, but a patio allows you to avoid getting your shoes and ankles soaked by wet grass, and provides a place to put garden furniture so you can sit and relax.

Creating walls that terrace a hillside, and patios that extend the living area of the house into the garden—these and other man-made constructions have their decorative as well as practical functions. By using decking and patios that come off the house and extend into the garden, you end up with the best of both worlds. I like these areas best when they are not totally separate; when parts of a patio or surfaced area impinge on the greenery, or, conversely, when areas of greenery overrun the boundaries of the patio and claim some of it for their own.

....

Opposite: The Nelson family's flat backyard in Lafayette, California, becomes multileveled and decorative through the use of a raised dais for a hot tub, with the vertical elements given emphasis by the rear wall of wood planks. The gardener uses 'Natalie Nypels' roses to soften the edge of the decking, and potted trees to soften the hard edges of the rear fence. Further interest is given by the tasteful use of the dark burgundy-leaved barberry and red-leaved Japanese maple in the background.

CHAPTER TWO

Fountains and Water Gardens

Of all the decorative elements in the garden, water is the most pleasing to the greatest number of people. Researchers studying human landscape preferences find that the two most desired landscape features, as reported by people from all over the world, are a large expanse of grass and water.

Water has always been associated with the source of life. The sight of a spring bubbling clear, cold, clean water onto a bed of gravel under the roots of a tree caused the ancient Europeans to people such spots with a variety of life-giving and sometimes life-threatening nymphs and spirits. Ancients believed that the four elements were earth, water, fire, and air—and certainly all four elements are necessary in the garden: the sun's fire for light and heat, the earth for soil and

stone, the air that supports life, and the water that is the basis of living tissue.

If you examine the structure of vegetation, you will see the appearance of flowing and swirling water hardened into wood as it forms the roots and twisting trunks of trees. Similarly, if you examine animal bone and tissue, you will also see reflections of the way that water flows. Life began in water, and the blood in our veins and the sap in the trees are some of that primeval ocean bound up in tissue and carried onto land, where its ebbs and flows create life. As a result, people from antiquity on have made water central to their creation myths.

The typical Spanish garden contains a fountain at its center carved in such a way that water is carried away in the four directions. This arrangement calls to mind

the Garden of Eden. "A river flowed from Eden to water the garden, and from there it divided to make four streams" (Gen. 2:10).

When you install a water feature in your garden, you will almost immediately see an increase in the life in your garden. You can stock your pool with fish to keep down mosquitoes, and the fish will add a bright flash to the water. There will be water plants: water lilies and lotuses; water irises, rushes, and papyrus. Soon the water striders will come—although how they arrive at your isolated pool of water will always be a mystery. The bees, mud daubers, and other insects will visit to take their drinks. A jeweled dragonfly will light on the leaves of the water plants. Birds will come to drink and play in the water. It's not unlikely that a frog or two will go a-courtin' by the waterside.

The sound of water's laughter, as when a brook plays over stones as it descends through a valley, is soothing to human ears. Still water was the first mirror, reflecting not only the person doing the looking, but also the heavens above.

Large pots without holes, containers with wide openings, even birdbaths, can function as water mirrors. These can be placed among the greenery and flowers in the garden, and are best elevated to about 3 or 4 feet (.9–1.2 m). As you walk through a garden, you'll notice that these water mirrors will reflect the silhouettes of the limbs above, with bright sky behind them; at night, they may reflect the moon and stars. They add a bit of mystery and magic to the garden, a feeling of ancient times.

In-ground pools of still water act as water mirrors, too. The great gardens at Château de Courances, south of Paris, are built around a series of reflecting pools, and one finds this kind of feature in most European and American classical gardens, from the Generalife above the Alhambra to the reflecting pool between the Washington Monument and the Lincoln Memorial in Washington, D.C.

Water certainly belongs in gardens meant to be places of beauty and abundance, and in fact, water will often dominate a garden, the way a candle on a table or fire in the fireplace will dominate a room. The eyes seem inexorably drawn to water in the garden, and the temptation is always to walk to the water's edge and peer over, to see what worlds might lurk beneath its surface.

Water becomes even more decorative and fun when you get it moving— although moving water should always be handled with taste and care. There's a fine line between a tasteful waterfall and an over-the-top fantasy. And do we all remember the fish fountain in Jacques Tati's movie *Mon Oncle*? It was a tacky fountain in the shape of a fish that was only turned on when the bourgeois owner deemed a visitor important enough.

Pools of Still Water

Lily Ponds in Containers

A lily pond is the ultimate garden decoration. The beauty of water lilies and lotuses (if you want to get fancy) is unsurpassed. Most gardeners only dream of having a lily pond, not realizing that it doesn't have to be elaborate.

A lily pond can be something as simple as a half barrel sunk into the ground to within a few inches of the soil surface. This is a good, if temporary, method of getting a water feature into your garden easily. The barrel will most likely last about 5 to 8 years, after which one or another of the staves will rot through, and you will come to the garden to discover your barrel empty and your water lily collapsed in the bottom. But you will have had many years of pleasure from it.

You can either replace it with a new half barrel, which is no big chore, actually, or with a ceramic pot. Ceramic pots can be partially buried or sit on top of the ground, where they function equally well. They won't rot through or leak if they aren't broken, and will serve for years, usually acquiring a patina as mosses get a toehold in accumulated surface smudges.

Ceramic pots used for this purpose should have a large opening on top. This opening provides ample surface for the plants to float their leaves upon.

In any case, if you are going to grow water lilies in containers, you need to keep several factors in mind. First, most water lilies bloom best in full sun. There are some shade-tolerant kinds that will bloom with as little as two hours of direct sunlight a day, but they will not bloom profusely. These varieties include 'Chromatella', a yellow type; 'Attraction' and 'Aflame', which are red; 'Masaniello', a pink variety; and 'Hal Miller', a white sort. These are all hardy water lilies. There are many tropicals of exquisite color, and the blue shades seem to bloom better with less sun than other colors— although again, full sun is best for the most bloom.

One of the chief suppliers of water plants in the United States is Lilypons Water Gardens (see Sources, page 187). The catalog has hundreds of varieties, as well as water pond equipment and instructions on how to plant water lilies in a pond or container.

Water lilies do not like moving water, so the water in your container should be still. No constantly dripping or running water should roil the surface. If you need to add water, submerge the end of the hose and gently top up the container.

Mosquitoes love to breed in containers full of still water, so you'll have to add a couple of fish to the container. Goldfish are easy to acquire; and when winter comes, you can bring them indoors to a fish tank. Many state environmental resources offices have mosquito-abatement divisions that will give you a few mosquito fish free of charge. These are small but voracious devourers of mosquito larvae.

As an alternative, you can control the larvae with *Bacillus thuringiensis* (Bt), a disease that affects only caterpillars and mosquito larvae. It's available at most garden centers and is harmless in the environment except to its targets; it will not poison dogs, cats, or birds that come to drink from your lily container. Simply add a small dash to each container

Left: *A pool of still water reinforces the quietude and stillness of the Arnold Steiner garden in Birmingham, Alabama. In the pool, water lilies* (Nymphaea) *open pure white blossoms that cup golden centers. Ivy and cotoneaster throw their slender stems down the brickwork that edges the pool, while in the background, a magnificent oakleaf hydrangea* (Hydrangea quercifolia) *spills its clusters of flowers in a white torrent over another brick wall.*

Page 32: *A lily pond, swimming pool, and hot tub are all included in this marvelously well designed terrace and garden on Long Island. With Long Island Sound in the background, the water surfaces repeat and echo each other. Notice how blue spruce, ornamental grasses, and worthy stones are arranged into miniature gardens set here and there around the pools.*

lilies won't bloom profusely in that corner, but the shade will give fish a place to hide, and the sight of a weeping tree dangling its branches in the water is always pretty.

Ponds are naturally more "at home" at the base of a slope than perched somewhere up on them. But be aware that nutrients also run downhill with rainwater or irrigation, and if they collect in your lily pond, you could get an algae bloom that will make your pond a gooey green mess. So make sure that lawn chemicals and fertilizers from the planting beds above can't get into your lily pond. If your pond must be on the slope, place it at the very top, or tuck it into a flat spot under a ledge or shelf if your slope has one.

Place the pond where it can be discovered. That means, avoid a site that can be seen from everywhere in the yard. It's much more fun and effective if people traversing your gardens suddenly discover a lily pond in full bloom. A secluded spot also makes the pond a nicer place to go for a moment's peace and solitude.

Once you've found the site, determine the size of the pool. Larger pools take more maintenance, which can include the installation of filtration systems. If this is your first pool, think smaller rather than larger, and then, when you've gained experience managing the pool, consider enlarging it or

monthly, or buy Mosquito Dunks, which are Bt added to a material that's pressed into doughnut shapes for use in large ponds. You can break off bits to add to the container monthly.

◉ Winter Handling of Tropical Water Lilies

Most gardeners in cold-winter climates either grow only hardy water lilies, or treat tropical lilies as annuals. But it is possible to overwinter tropical lilies indoors—and certainly cheaper than buying new ones each year (see pages 170–71).

The tropicals are wonderful plants, with blooms all summer into fall. They come in the most evocative colors, are sweetly fragrant, and generally have larger flowers than the hardy lilies.

◉ In-Ground Lily Ponds

An in-ground lily pond requires a commitment. You need to construct it and landscape it in a way that's pleasing (see pages 171–73). You need to create a small but functioning healthy ecosystem so it doesn't turn into an algae pit. And if you are growing tropical lilies and lotuses, you'll have to bring them indoors for the winter.

Before you begin the installation process, the most important decision you need to make is where to site the pond. Plan for a location with full sun, or close to full sun. Since the purpose of the pond is to show off the beauty of water lily blossoms, remember that the more sun, the more blooms. If a quarter or less of the pond falls under the shade of an overhanging tree, that's ideal. Perhaps the

building another, bigger one. A minimum-size pool, however, would be 3 feet by 5 feet on its surface and 3 feet deep at the center (1 x 1.5 x 1 m). You could grow two or three lilies in such a pool, because you want at least two-thirds of the surface covered with leaves. A pool of this size would give you 15 square feet (1.5 m²) of surface, with 10 square feet (1 m²) covered by leaves. You want that much coverage because the leaves intercept the sunlight; too much sun penetrating will cause ugly algae blooms.

If your pond does experience an algae bloom, you'll find it hard to get rid of, short of emptying the pond and sterilizing it. Exercise caution up front by considering possible problems and prevention techniques.

Algae blooms are caused by too many nutrients in the water. You can grow submerged aquatic plants, or oxygenating plants, which soak up nutrients and release oxygen into the water. Aquatic plant nurseries sell many different types of submerged aquatics, which provide habitat and oxygen for fish as well as help keep things clean.

Opposite: *No expense was spared to create this in-ground lily pool at a private garden in Santa Barbara, California—but the result is worth it. The raised portion of beautifully dressed stone is like a good frame on a painting, setting it off and enhancing the jewel-like beauty of the pool and its flowers. Roses,* Lavandula stoechas, *and* Tulbaghia *maintain the elegant, subdued theme.*

Below: *The simplicity of this decorative pond, stocked with water lilies* (Nymphaea) *and lotus* (Nelumbo), *contrasts beautifully with the sheer lush exuberance of the plantings that surround it. It was designed by Tish Rehill for a client in Southampton, New York.*

You certainly will need fish for mosquito control, but use restraint. Too many fish will spell trouble, because overproduction of nitrogen-rich feces will cause the dreaded algae bloom. A good rule of thumb is to measure "inches of fish"—you will want about two-thirds to three-fourths of an inch (1.5 to 2 cm) of fish for every square foot (30 cm^2) of water surface. So, if you have 15 square feet (1.5 m^2), keep the number of "fish inches" to about 10 or 11 (or 4 to 4.5 "fish centimeters").

The number of fish is less important than the cumulative size of the fish load; that's why the rule is given in inches of fish. If you buy 2-inch (5-cm) goldfish, you would stock your 3 x 5–foot (.9 x 1.5–m) pond with no more than five or six fish. As they grow, you will need to reduce their number to maintain the proportion.

Building codes usually require that ponds more than 3 feet deep (90 cm) be fenced in, to prevent accidental drowning. That's why most lily ponds are a shallow 2 to 3 feet (60 to 90 cm) deep. Actually, most pools range through both depths, as the typical construction method involves a three-foot-deep (90-cm-deep) center with a one- or two-foot-deep (30- or 60-cm-deep) shelf all the way around. Some aquatic plants will sit on the shelf, others on the deep bottom. All will be in pots.

To allow easy management and handling of aquatic plants, pot them up in rich soil, then cover the soil surface with a couple of inches (5 cm) of fine gravel before submerging them. The gravel keeps the soil particles from floating away. Since the plants are in pots, they can be easily brought up for removal

Watercourses on a property, such as this one at the Barbara Barnett garden, designed by Craig Luna, in Jonesboro, Georgia, are pretty but need to be traversed if visitors are to see its wonders up close. Here the designer has opted for the simplicity and elegance of a simple rounded footbridge that takes the visitor to a wooden plank path. Thus the focus stays on the water, the hostas, and the nicely placed junipers in the background.

of spent stems and flower stalks, or for moving to a new spot.

Materials for Submerged Portions of Pools

Since pool liners are black, they absorb most of the light entering the pool. So when you look into the water, it's hard to tell how deep the water is, or that it's lined with a fabricated liner. When it's brand-new, there may be some shine off the liner that gives it away, but the liner soon becomes dulled and very natural looking as particles of mud deposit on it.

You can add some materials down in the water to reflect light and bits of color, such as a few hand mirrors or colored glass, but unless you have positive filtration for your water, mud, drowned dust particles, and the normal detritus that settles out in a pond will soon cover their surface as they lie on the bottom.

For that reason, if you want to put something that sparkles at the bottom of your pool, place it in a dark or black plastic tray that you can easily retrieve. Then hose off the bits of glass or mirror before submerging the tray again.

Innovative Ways to Decorate Natural Lake and Pond Sites

Folks lucky enough to have a natural stream, pond, or lake on their property are confronted with the challenge of an overabundance of ways to approach landscaping. In the final analysis, because the water itself is such a strong feature, simplicity is the best way to go.

A Japanese-style bamboo waterspout produces its mechanical motions by the side of a built waterfall in Portland, Oregon. The upper bamboo stem carries a trickle of water to the larger, lower one, and slowly fills it. When the bottom one fills sufficiently, it pivots on its axle and pours its water into the stream, then rights itself.

A bath house or cabana, if the water can be used for swimming, can make a charming addition to a lakeside beach. An outdoor patio and bar near the water gives people a place to sit and enjoy the view. If there's a large tree nearby, a swing that arcs out over the water is fun for all who use it. If the water is deep enough, it makes a fine launching pad for a big splash.

Large stones can be used to make a jetty. A path can run down the top so people can walk out into the water; place soil between stones and plant the jetty with low-growing charmers like forget-me-nots and primroses for the spring, followed by verbenas and other flowers that bloom all summer.

Constructing a terrace wall that plunges into the water will give gardeners the opportunity to plant ferns or other moisture-loving plants between the stones so they make a cascade down the wall's face. The interface between water below and garden beds above the wall can be softened with water irises or reeds emerging from the shallows near the wall to meet these cascading plants.

Give your pond or stream a vertical dimension by a careful, artistic arrangement of beautiful stones that protrude above the water. Think of the water's surface as the soil surface, and place very large stones so that their weightiest portion is down and they are submerged to at least a third or even two-thirds of their height. If they are not water-washed, but have hard, angular features, site them so that they appear to be an extension of the same forces that have created rocky upheavals nearby. If you have a flat landscape without massive rock upthrusting, consider a quiet arrangement of rounded rocks. By all means plant water lilies or water grasses with the stones.

Edging for ponds and streams is best when diverse. Stones or bricks keep feet dry during rainy weather. Grass looks beautiful when it runs to the water's edge. Tall reeds or shrubbery lend interest to the pond border. Large boulders set right at the pond edge and extending into the water give visitors a place to sit and think. Several of these edgings used together give a more natural and inviting appearance than just one used around the entire circumference. Statues or art set either directly into water or on a pedestal in the water gives the artwork the finest of settings, as the water will strongly attract the gaze and deliver the eye to the artwork.

Finally, a drowned building or ruin is a wonderful effect. This can be something as simple as a partial wall running down into the water, covered over with flowering vines.

Moving Water

Recirculating Water

If nothing decorates the garden like water, then no water is more decorative than moving water. Unless you have a natural waterfall or stream on your property, you need a submersible water pump to achieve the effect.

Submersible pumps are at the heart of most moving water features in the garden. They are typically attached to 115-volt house current in the United States. You can use them to filter and aerate water in your pond, to drive a fountain, to pump recirculating water from a catch-basin pond to the top of a waterfall, or to recirculate water in a moving stream back to the source.

To determine the right size pump, you first must know how much water you have in your pond or system. At the small

end, a $1/250$ horsepower (2.8 W) pump will recirculate about a gallon (3.8 l) of water a minute to the top of a 5-foot (1.5 m) rise, and will cost around 60 dollars. That's hardly more than a trickle, and it's designed for ponds of less than 350 gallons (1.32 kl).

At the big end, a $1/2$ horsepower (350 W) pump will move about a gallon of water each second to a height of 5 feet and cost about 400 dollars. It's designed for ponds of from 2,000 to 3,000 gallons (7.6–11 kl).

There are more than a dozen sizes of pumps between these extremes, so you'll be able to fit one to your pond size fairly closely.

Submersible pumps are primarily designed for waterfalls and artificial streams, either with or without filtration. If you have the right size pump with a filter system, and get a diverse ecosystem established in your pond, you probably won't have much trouble with algae blooms and rank, soupy water. Even without filtration, rank water is fairly easy to avoid when you're moving the water constantly and there's a diverse ecosystem in place.

....

In Barbara Poole's garden in Portola Valley, California, formal terracing and brickwork mix easily with natural-looking arrangements of water-smoothed stones in an inviting pool. Grasses, artemisias, and roses soften the setting. The designer has made the pool on two levels, connected by flagstone terracing, with two very decorative waterfalls suggesting how the stones came to be so smooth. The result is irresistible.

For sheer aeration, specially designed pumps will blast water into tiny droplets thrown high in the air. This aerates and cleans pond water, and is especially beneficial if you're raising fish.

A solar-operated pump is an option. I once had a small pond with a submersible pump run off two solar panels hidden away around the side of the house. It was less than ideal. The water only circulated—and thus I only had my waterfall—during the hours of maximum sunlight. Since this was when I was working, I had little time to enjoy the waterfall. Not only that, but the panels barely produced enough electric current to get the pump moving, and the water was hard to get started. There was usually a lot of hose priming going on. Eventually, I put a new pump on house current and was much more satisfied, if not as environmentally correct.

Any licensed electrician can install your service through a metal conduit to the submersible pump so that it meets existing local building codes for outdoor electrical work. It's a good idea to put the on-off switch in an all-weather housing on an outside wall of the house, so that you can turn it on as you walk out to the garden and turn it off as you return.

It's also a good idea to put your pump inside a pump protector—a heavy-duty plastic mesh container that keeps leaves and debris from being sucked into the pump intake, where they can clog the pump, cut down on the amount of water drawn in, and make the pump work too hard, which shortens its life.

If you're concerned about the cost of electricity for a pump, first decide the size of the pump you need. It will be rated as to watts used. The small unit mentioned above rates about 20 watts, while the big $1/2$ HP unit draws 1100 watts. Multiply the number of watts by an estimated number of hours you'll run the pump each month. If your pump draws 100 watts and you run it two hours a day, that's about 6,000 watt-hours per month. Divide this figure by 1,000 to get the number of kilowatt-hours used each month. In this case, that's 6 kilowatt-hours. Electricity is sold by the kilowatt-hour, so check with your local power company for the cost of a kilowatt-hour of power in your area. Multiply the cost of a kilowatt by 6 to see how much running the pump for 2 hours a day will add to your monthly electrical bill. Currently, a kilowatt-hour in my area runs about a dime, so running a 100-watt pump for a couple of hours a day is going to cost 60 cents. Even the biggest pump will cost only about 7 or 8 dollars for 2 hours a day. Of course, electricity from the solar panels costs nothing, but the panels are very expensive.

Recirculating pumps can also be used to circulate water through Japanese flumes. A flume is made from an upright piece of bamboo into which another piece of bamboo, the spout, is inserted at right angles near the top of the upright. A small pump is adequate as water generally trickles from the spout into a basin carved from stone. The basin may be set on rocks through which the water flows downward to a holding tank, where it is recirculated up through the upright bamboo to the spout.

A variation of this idea is to replace the spout with a piece of horizontal bamboo that pivots on a swivel, weighted so that it is tilted slightly upward when empty. This bamboo shaft remains horizontal while filling with water, but when the water reaches a certain weight, the bamboo tips downward and the water gushes out. It then rights itself and the process begins again.

Those with large ponds in mild climates might consider stocking the ponds with koi, a Japanese breed of carp valued for their beautiful variegated colors. The word *koi* means "living flowers," and these very beautiful fish live up to the term. They can survive in cold climates, but if the pond freezes over, the ice must be removed so oxygen can dissolve in the water—which effectively limits them to zones 8 and warmer in the United States, or regions where the minimum winter temperature doesn't go much below 15 to 20 degrees Fahrenheit (–10 to –7°C). In summer when temperatures rise, they need a shady spot where the water remains cool. These fish are social animals and enjoy swimming in schools, so it's important to stock your pond with at least a dozen fish. They do grow large, however—up to 4 feet (120 cm) long after many decades—and so you need enough room so that each 10 inches of fish in your pond has at least a square yard of water surface (or about a square meter for every 25 cm of fish).

◙ Waterwheels

Waterwheels are fun to see in action, spinning when water in the holding sections builds to a weight that pushes the wheel downward. There are two principal designs, overshot and undershot.

The overshot wheel receives its water from above, filling its holding sections one at a time. In days before steam power, overshot wheels were used to grind grain and were usually placed below a dam. The water level behind the dam would rise high enough that a sluice could carry the overflow and dump it on the top of the wheel. As the sections filled, their weight would turn the wheel, the wheel would turn a shaft, and the shaft would be attached to gears that would transfer the torque to the millstones.

The undershot wheel extends paddle blades down into a moving stream, and the weight of the moving water against the paddles turns the wheels. They're also fun decorations in the water garden if you have a moving stream, but not quite as dramatic looking as the overshot wheel.

Your waterwheel doesn't have to turn millstones. You could simply use the wheel for decoration and not harness the action at all.

Because the stones are arranged to carry the water widely over the surface of this waterfall, it has a greater presence than one single fall of water. Mosses soften the stones, and water plants grow in the pond below. A pot of red impatiens adds a needed touch of color. This feature decorates the garden of Craig Luna in Riverdale, Georgia.

◉ Wishing Wells

If you are going to decorate your garden with a wishing well, let me encourage you to do it where there is a real spring, so that it is a functioning well. Otherwise it's just a gimcrack (see page 173).

This is quite a project by the time you're finished, but if it's truly a functioning spring well, it's a legitimate and classy addition to a garden site. You might want to make a small sign asking folks not to throw money in the well if you plan to drink from it.

◉ Built Streams and Channels

A natural-looking stream can be built much like a recirculating water pond, except that the pond is stretched out into a stream. While a stream can be made any length, 15 to 25 feet (5–8 m) is a good size for most gardens and yards, as it keeps the pump requirement within reason.

The stream can be relatively flat, with water entering the pump at one end, traveling back to the other end in a buried pipe or hose, and then beginning the journey over again. This produces a gently moving stream that will produce some movement in reeds, irises, or water grasses that are planted in pots and submerged in the water.

You can also fashion a stream so that there is a series of shallow rocky falls alternating with relatively level places where the water is smooth. If you choose this option, stagger the distances between the rapids and vary the lengths of the still-water sections to keep it looking natural. Try to keep the total rise from bottom to top no more than 5 feet (1.5 m), so the pump can adequately move enough water back to the top for the rapids to look realistic. The higher the rise, the less water the pump will be able to move. If there's barely a trickle coming down over the shallow rapids, you will lose the effect and increase the possibility that algae, like the long strands of slimy spirogyra, will develop. Remember that still water should be deeper and the rapids relatively shallow.

You will need a liner, laid out in a long meander. The edges of the stream should be a varied mix of many different sizes of rocks and clumps of waterside plants that cover the liner where it's folded onto a shallow shelf just below ground level. The effect will be much more natural if you choose rocks and stones of one type, rather than having many different textures and colors of stone.

Another possibility is to construct channels that will carry moving water around the garden in geometric patterns. These channels are best if they are narrow, deeper than wide, and lined with brick. The brick hides the thick flexible liner that's always necessary when creating water features.

It's delightful to see water coursing along straight, man-made channels through a garden, whether a minimalist garden that echoes the spare feeling of the channels, or a natural-looking garden that contrasts with the built quality of the channels.

You can make these channels turn at severe angles, right angles, or swing around a semicircular bend. They look best when the water is made to follow defined, mathematical shapes. Their purpose? Sheer decoration. But moving water is living water, and is a very attention-getting element in a quiet garden that only moves when the wind touches it.

◉ Waterfalls of Surpassing Beauty

A stack of big, blocky rocks piled up on a flat yard, with a stream of water pouring over the lip of the top rock, has no relationship to reality. Why would a pile of rocks be in the yard in the first place? And why would a stream of water be pouring from the top of the pile? It just looks ludicrous.

Waterfalls, to be beautiful, have to be integrated into your site. If your yard is flat, you'll need to give it some contour, such as a bank or berm, and then work the waterfall into the slope. After all, water falls because it's running downhill—which means there has to be a hill.

Nevertheless, a waterfall doesn't have to be high or massive to be beautiful. It can pour in pretty sheets from a wide, low shelf of rock just a foot or so high. Even a waterfall as low as 6 inches (15 cm) will make a happy, burbling sound, an ornament in any garden (see pages 173–74).

When constructing naturalistic waterfalls, I like to go to the source: I look for hills where water is flowing down slopes, and I take along a notebook. When I find a waterfall—even a small one—of surpassing beauty, I sketch its appearance and layout, including the degree of slope, plant placement, and

how the rocks of all sizes are placed. These sketch notes have been invaluable to me, for they constantly give me ideas.

One thing I have noticed is that you never see the source of a stream. It always winds away out of sight somewhere above you. So when building a waterfall, remember to hide the source of the water around a curve behind a rock.

I once saw a waterfall just a couple of feet high, but very pretty. Winter and spring torrents had washed away most of the soil from the rock assemblage in the streambed and along its sides, but had exposed a twisting, gnarled root that insinuated itself among the big stones, appearing and disappearing like an anaconda in the forest.

When I dug out a bank for a waterfall a few months later, a large root of a nearby oak tree was exposed. I asked the workmen to be careful with it, to excavate the soil from about 5 feet (1.5 m) of its length, and then worked the design of the stones around it, keeping in mind how the water would run and echoing the root's solid liquidity with the water's cavorting path down the slope. The result

Fine rockwork and good design make this an extraordinary swimming pool, combining a series of waterfalls and several discrete bathing areas with pretty terracing and lush garden plantings. How much nicer than a simple, flat, featureless in-ground pool. The superb construction here in the Moss family garden in Saugus, California, integrates pool, garden, and patio into one overall scene, and the sound of the falling water blocks any street noise that might reach this idyllic spot.

Right: Twenty jets of water produce a spectacular display of sound and motion at Long Vue Gardens in New Orleans. When not turned on, the fountain is a peaceful and quiet reflecting pool, but when the jets are operating it's a lively show. The surrounding garden's formal design is emphasized by the fountain's grace and simplicity.

Opposite: Although the look of this choice spot is casual, it all follows fairly rigorous rules for creating a Japanese stone garden with a water basin. The garden, in Lake Oswego, Oregon, evokes the idea of an oasis in the wilderness where a traveler can find a refreshing drink. The rectangular stone in the foreground is the place where the pilgrim stands. The water is carried to the basin (a particularly fine example, by the way) through a traditional bamboo pipe. Azaleas and Japanese maples suggest the forest through which the pilgrim is traveling.

was unexpectedly pretty; the oak's living presence enhanced the stone and water around it.

A set of stone steps flanking the waterfall and leading up the slope can be made of the same type of stone and look inviting and natural.

◙ Combination Swimming Pool and Waterfall

An acquaintance of mine combined a swimming pool with waterfalls in the cleverest way. Behind his house, the flat lawn stretched toward a rather steep upward slope. He put in a rectangular swimming pool on the flat lawn, with the far short side, at the deep end, built back into the hill. The pool cement and tiles rose vertically and disappeared into a tier of huge boulders, carefully placed

and partially buried, so that they looked like they had always been there. One could dive off the flat top of the lowest boulder into the pool.

Running the whole length of the long, right side of the pool were five broad steps that began below water level. These generous steps ended under more huge boulders worked into the hillside and planted all around with greenery.

A push of a button allowed water to flow onto the diving boulder at the back end of the pool, off its flat top, and into the pool in a graceful waterfall. More water coursed out in a long, flat sheet onto the top step at the right side of the pool and flowed off it onto the next step, then down onto the next, and finally into the pool, turning the steps into a series of waterfalls that ended by splashing gaily into the pool water.

◙ Natural Streams

Having a natural year-round stream on your property affords you great opportunities for creativity.

Before you change one whit of it, however, you should check with your

state and local departments of environmental resources, fish and wildlife, and other agencies to make sure that any changes will not disturb valuable habitat or endanger existing stocks of fish. Straightening channels can also cause water to flow more rapidly, scouring out banks and causing erosion. Clearing brush can expose the water to more sunlight, heating it and causing environmental changes that will translate into ecological changes.

Putting in a dam with a waterfall spillway is a fine idea and will create more diverse habitat, but it also will slow water flow and possibly increase water temperature. It's important to know the effects of a dam on water quality.

If you get the okay to divert or change a stream, you might consider separating its flow into two or more channels. One channel can run over a waterfall, another may fill a dammed pond that acts as bass pond for fishing, swimming hole, and reflecting pool, then flow over the spillway and run down to rejoin the stream where it exits your property. Or you may leave the stream as it is and build bridges and stepping stones over and through it.

Fountains

◙ Sprays and Jets

During the Renaissance, the aristocrats of Italy, Germany, and England used the principles of water sprays and jets to play tricks on their guests. Visitors to grand

estates would wander into grottoes and outdoor rooms furnished with stone tables and benches, unaware that the lord of the place had riddled the furniture with wormhole-size tunnels connected to pressurized sources of water. When the guests were busy chatting, the lord high prankster would turn the handles and open the water spouts. As the French essayist Montaigne's secretary noted in his journal on a trip in 1580 to Villa Pratolino, Francesco de' Medici's Tuscan estate, suddenly "the whole grotto is full of water, and all the seats squirt water on your buttocks; and if you flee from the grotto and climb the castle stairs, there come out of every other step of the stairs, right to the top of the house, a thousand jets of water that give you a bath."

Given the bathing practices of the time, perhaps this was Francesco's way of improving the atmosphere.

Sprays and jets are still fun, although today we seldom use them to ambush our guests. Now we confine them to decorative garden pools and water features, where they take many shapes. In modern designs, they often simply shoot from jet nozzles in arcs, sometimes intersecting,

....

Two beautiful metal waterbirds double as fountains in Jeanne Lipsitt's garden in Norcross, Georgia. The grace of the birds is matched by the graceful way in which the Japanese maple (Acer palmatum 'Dissectum Atropurpureum') in the background holds its filigreed foliage. The mossy banks and variegated swordlike leaves of the potted water plant complete the subtle beauty of the scene.

Left: *This wonderful bit of decoration at the Rediker family garden in Birmingham, Alabama, began as a stone wall with a shallow niche in it. A simple wooden archway was attached as a frame for an elaborate cast stone recirculating fountain. Then potted yellow mandevilla vines were set on either side of the fountain, giving life and color to the scene. The result is a captivating decoration for a plain wall.*

Below: *A private garden in Seattle surrounds a very decorative centerpiece, with a sculptured metal fountain set in a concrete pool. The flagstones around the pool help define the space further, and the small plantings between the flagstones soften the fountain. The rest of the yard is handled with a severe formality that the fountain enlivens.*

A fountain that bubbles out of the ground suggests the fertility of the earth. Here a millstone, also suggestive of fruitfulness, is used as the centerpiece. The water drains into a catch basin below the stones and is recirculated up through the center of the millstone. The effect is riveting. This is a superior decoration for any garden.

sometimes in rows, and sometimes in single jets. Each jetted stream makes a sound as the water lands, and it is possible to adjust the length of the spray to make each jet sound a different note, and even to harmonize those notes into a water symphony. Most often, though, the chief effect is visual, and denotes abundance — a plenitude of water to sustain life.

In older gardens, as well as in modern ones that hark back to former times, statuary is configured to spray water from animal and human figures. Often the water jets emerge from the mouth, but no orifice is off-limits to the water sculptor, and the figure of a woman with stone breasts shooting jets of water is common, while the little boy relieving himself in a pool is so common it's a cliché.

The fountains of the 17th, 18th, and 19th centuries, and especially those of the Victorian era, were devoted to sprays. One artful example is the life-size figure of a triton, carved by Caius Gabriel Cibber about 1690, for the fourth earl of Devonshire, at Chatsworth, in Derbyshire. The triton is sounding his horn, as if giving voice to the strong jets that spray water many feet high all around him.

Of course, among classic uses of water are André Le Nôtre's monumental creations at Versailles and the whole hillside of jets and sprays issuing from balustrades, stairways, and sculpture at the 16th-century Villa Lante at Viterbo, north of Rome.

With the demise of the aristocracy and the wealth they had to create elaborate water features, most of today's jet and spray creations are in public fountains and plazas, and around corporate headquarters. But that doesn't mean that a homeowner with a strong pump and jet nozzles can't create some interesting effects in the landscape. Jets can be aimed to cover a piece of statuary with water, or to simply throw high in the air exuberant streams of water that tinkle musically as they fall back into the pool.

In hot climates, nozzles that spray very fine mists are used to cool down guests at lawn parties. Typically a tent will be set up over one of the mist-pumps, and people can walk in for a refreshing mist bath that further cools as it evaporates off the skin.

Fountains

When we think of garden fountains, most of us think of old-fashioned fountains with a basin, perhaps in the shape of an opened, upturned seashell, and a central portion that may be a figure or may be several tiers of basins in diminishing sizes down which the water courses.

Such arrangements, usually made of cast concrete, are easy to find at many outlets that sell traditional garden furnishings. A recirculating pump is placed in a housing under the base, and the water needs to be replenished every so often to replace the amount lost through evaporation.

If you choose to put in a traditional deep fountain, be very sure that it will not pose a hazard to small children who could fall in.

There are so many other delightful types of garden fountains that we needn't stop with the traditional. Almost any solid structure of stone or concrete that has a hole through the center can be used to create a fountain; an effective example is a millstone fountain (see pages 174–75).

Pillars with holes down their centers also make good bubbling fountains, with the water gushing out of the top of the

....

Water gently flows down over the surface of this sculpted fountain in Erika Shank's garden in Amagansett, New York. It turns a static sculpture into a shimmering treat. The water flows through the blue-gray beach cobbles into a receptacle under the sculpture and is recirculated. The designer has artfully placed the fountain within a small grove of poplar trees, and thoughtfully provided a viewing stone on which to stand.

pillar and spilling over its surface, eventually making a nice patina evoking antiquity. Such bubbling pillars are best set back into foliage that partially covers them.

This is an area of garden decoration that calls for creativity. Keep your eyes open for stone or concrete pieces with holes in them, or find a stone you love and have a local quarry drill it out. Or you may decide to fit three stones together, like a lithic version of the three graces, and run a water pipe up the center between them where it can't be seen. No drilling is required, and the water can course down over the stones, adding a dynamic new dimension to their static beauty.

Bog Gardens

An advantage of having a natural pond is that the margins of the pond are perfect for bog plants, which include some of the most imposing and beautiful plants in the garden. *Eupatorium maculatum* and *Filipendula rubra* are two lovely examples of bog-loving perennials.

In the built water garden, however, the pond is defined by the flexible liner underneath. Just as it's possible to build a pond, it's also possible to build a bog—and in much the same way (see pages 175–76).

....

Natural water- or bog-loving plants find a perfect home along the edge of this small pond in Ellen Coster's garden, designed by Connie Cross, in Cutchogue, New York. They include the small lavender Myosotis, *the grass mounds of miscanthus, hostas, and the true water plant,* Eichhornia crassipes, *blooming as it floats in the back of the pond.*

CHAPTER THREE

Walls, Fences, and Gates

Walls and fences are separators in the garden, but in a strange, backhanded way, they also pull the garden together. On a large property without walls and fences, it would be difficult to integrate all the areas of the property into a unified whole. With everything visible at once, the gardener would have to relate everything to just one theme to keep the property visually manageable. I prefer a garden with several small spaces. It's more fun to devise a whole new scheme for each space than to have to subject everything to the property's single grand scheme.

Walls and fences are usually placed without a great deal of consideration for garden design. Their placement is ordinarily utilitarian. In Europe centuries ago, gardens behind the main house were walled to keep the livestock (and any passing human pilferers) from eating the produce. I remember once tramping along paths in France, finding a wall running through an overgrown woods. I surmised that it was once part of the *clos* that defined a garden. As I walked on, the woods thinned out and the wall emerged to run up to the back of a gorgeous Francis I–style country house. The woods, I then noticed, were an overgrown hazel brake; the remains of the three *clos* walls (the back of the house served as the fourth wall) were clearly visible.

Fences are also usually set for practical purposes, such as marking the boundaries of a piece of property, along a street, or between neighbors. In the garden, however, walls and fences can exist solely to separate the garden into discrete spaces, and to hide one part of the garden from the next. A wall may be constructed as part of a terraced slope, or as a place for plants to tumble and spread. A fence may keep the garden explorer moving in the direction intended by the gardener, so that, rounding a bend in the path, the visitor is given an unexpected view of a well-designed and executed piece of the gardener's art.

Gates, of course, keep people out— but they also let people in. A massive gate, unadorned and locked, says Keep Out about as forcefully as possible. An open gate, on the other hand, ringed with flowers and overtopped with an arbor spun with clematis 'Perle d'Azur' and climbing red roses, says Come In as charmingly as if the gardener were standing there with hand outstretched.

Walls

How to Choose a Style of Wall

Before you choose a style of wall that's right for your garden, you need to spend a moment deciding the purposes of the wall. Ask yourself what the practical purposes are. Will the wall separate the property from the street, blocking off the world outside and helping to block out street noise as well? Will the wall separate one level of the garden from another, or one discrete garden area from another? Will it create privacy for a patio or swimming or sunbathing area? Will it define a place for barbeques, lawn bowling, or bocce? Will it block the offending view of a neighbor's neglected shack, or of a driveway? A stone garden wall can shelter the garden plot from cold winds, and it can soak up the sun's heat during the day and radiate it at night to prolong the gardening season and hasten bloom.

The wall may have more than one practical purpose. For instance, a wall might be built perpendicular to a long, straight pathway, which puts a sudden stop to the eye as it travels down the path, giving a focal point for the setting. And this same wall might divide the garden into a planting area with a garden path on one side and a patio area on the other.

Decide if the wall has any ornamental purposes. Will it function as the backdrop for forward plantings? Do you plan to surmount it with formal, classical ornamentation such as urns and pots? Will plants grow over it or up it, or spill down its sides?

Finally, calculate the aesthetic purposes of the wall. By that I mean how it will fit in with the materials on the property, such as the construction of the house, of other existing walls and fences, of materials in the pathway, of either naturally occurring or placed stones. If the house is brick, a wall that abuts the house and becomes part of its design might best be brick also. Will the wall be a backdrop for plants or a stage for them, or a pedestal for potted plants?

Once you've decided on the wall's practical, ornamental, and aesthetic purposes, you can best choose some of the features of the wall—whether it should be a dry wall, made of mortared stone, block, or brick; how high it should be and how it should be finished. And then you can think about touches that might add indi-

Left: *What a splendid entrance to a garden! Flat stones make a lovely wall that's made far less forbidding by the wrought-iron openwork on either side of the gateposts. The posts themselves are topped with finials cast in a bud theme. White tulips and bits of color endear themselves to visitors who walk this path at Jim Gibbs's garden in Ball Ground, Georgia.*

Page 54: *'Joseph's Coat' roses smother a beautiful example of a classic colonial picket fence at a private residence in Los Angeles. The posts with their urn-shaped finials and the square pickets that pierce the horizontal crosspieces all add to the crisp, luxurious effect. The roses alleviate the severe classicity of the fence by splashing it with ice-cream colors.*

viduality and interest to the wall: could there be a niche for a statue, or a spot for a fountain? Should the wall be topped with flat stones of a color that contrasts with the basic wall?

Speaking of mortared walls, no introduction to such walls can go by without remembering one of the most famous walls of all—the one for which Shakespeare wrote a part in "A Midsummer Night's Dream." Tom Snout the tinker plays the wall in Shakespeare's hilarious play-within-a-play "A Tedious Brief Scene of Young Pyramus and His Love Thisbe; Very Tragical Mirth." Thisbe, waiting for her lover Pyramus to arrive on the other side, says to the wall, "My cherry lips have often kissed thy stones, thy stones with lime and hair knit up in thee." Well, that's an unappetizing kiss. But it does indicate how mortar was made in Shakespeare's day.

◙ Dry Walls

When I lived in Pennsylvania, I had a friend who was a marvelous stonemason. He built the most beautiful stone walls—both dry (without mortar) and vertical walls with mortar. When he had finished a wall, he would stand back, look at it with satisfaction, and say, "Every stone a picture."

His talent inspired me to try my hand at a dry wall. I found a spot that needed a retaining wall to terrace and hold a steep bank of loose soil. There were two huge boulders already at the bottom of the bank, which I used as my anchor stones.

At one end of my property was an old stone row made by farmers over the centuries, who had cleared stones from these fields, dragging them to the edges of the fields on horse-drawn sledges called stone boats and heaping them into rows.

Now the stone rows were overgrown with poison ivy and Virginia creeper. Out of them grew chokecherry, wild hazelnuts, and sassafras hung with wild grapes—a rich habitat for many of the birds and furry animals of rural Pennsylvania. A short section of one of these massive old rock piles became my source of materials for the dry wall.

If you aren't lucky enough to have indigenous stone to work with, building

The open gate at Mary Matthews's garden in White Oak, South Carolina, is made friendly and inviting by its crown of pink 'Constance Spry' roses, and the ivy and violets that soften the footpath of brick.

Left: *Well-made dry walls of stone will stand for centuries, even though they have no mortar. This premier example is in the village of Blockley in Gloucestershire, England. It's graced along its bottom course by the opportunistic perennial* Centranthus ruber, *which often associates with dry places, limestone walls, or even the alkaline soil around decayed mortared walls.*

Opposite: *The wall at Bill Slater's garden in Santa Barbara, California, is finished with a smooth, ocher-tinted plaster of cement, giving a subtle backdrop for a busy border that contains a beautifully formed cypress in a huge pot. If the wall was visually busy, the free-form shape of the cypress would be harder to see.*

materials suppliers usually carry many different kinds of stone. Use ones that appeal to you, but make sure they have chunky sides so they stack well, and are all of the same type and color of stone, although the patinas may vary. Some people like the look of a wall made of rounded cobbles of the kind retrieved from river outwashes, but these stones don't appeal to me. Cobbles are almost impossible to stack, and even built up into a wall, never look natural to my eye. They have a decorative quality, to be sure, but in an arts-and-craftsy way. My idea of the classic stone wall is one made of naturally chunky rocks, the kind I retrieved from the old stone row that was my quarry.

After several weeks of working at my dry wall for an hour or two a day, I came to know why my mason friend never lifted a rock, but always hired young men to do

so. My back was in terrible shape. Yes, this is a caveat for you, dear reader. If you intend to build stone walls, either learn how to lift properly or hire some people who can do it without injuring themselves. And, whether it's you or your workers, always use a back brace that cinches around the waist and supports both abdominal and lower-back muscles. As I found out, it is not macho to lift stones without precautions—it is stupid. The reason my mason friend never lifted a stone is that he simply couldn't do it anymore. His back had been blown out years before.

Despite this drawback, I encourage you to build your own dry wall. It's a very earthy and satisfying experience. No wall looks better in the garden than a well-built dry wall. No wall will last longer. And it is meditative work, because you can't rush the process without ruining the result (see pages 176–79).

Stucco-Finished and Concrete Walls

Many old 18th- and 19th-century farmhouses in the eastern United States were made of native dressed stone by artisans who labored long and hard to give the finished walls the most decorative look. Later, however, many of these stone houses were stuccoed over to stabilize the aging mortared joints and to help keep them weathertight. Now, of course, present-day owners of these homes go to great expense to have the stucco chipped away and expose the stonework again.

I tell this by way of suggesting that stucco should be applied to stonework only if it will improve its appearance. There are situations that call out for stuccoing.

For example, a simple but not very aesthetic way to build a stone wall is to set

Left: *Bricks can be used in almost infinite patterns. This fine specimen of a brick wall is installed in Anne Carr's garden in Atlanta. It includes a shelf, two columns with recessed interiors, a decorative course along the top, and staggered walls of brick and empty spaces. The formal effect is enhanced by the large leaves of* Hosta sieboldiana *on either side of the Chinese pot.*

Opposite: *Here's a stone wall designed by artist Dan Snow, where every stone in the wall and the cap contributes to the oceanic swell and flow of the composition. Garden designer Gordon Hayward does justice to the wall by topping it with a dwarf Norway spruce (*Picea abies *'Nidiformis') that spills and flows over it, recapitulating the movement of the stones. The sea of blue-green* Juniperus sabina var. tamariscifolia *at the lower left adds to the effect. The garden is in New Hampshire.*

up wooden forms, as you would for cast concrete, pour in a layer of wet concrete, then dump in a layer of stone, then another layer of concrete, another layer of stone, and so on until the wall reaches the top of the form. When the concrete sets up and the forms are removed, the resulting wall looks as though rubble were haphazardly set into concrete—which is pretty much what has occurred. Such walls are, I believe, candidates for stuccoing.

Similarly, concrete block walls are easy to build, go up quickly, and are relatively inexpensive; they are also—unless you are using some of the more decorative and expensive precast concrete blocks— not very attractive. But a sturdy wall can be quickly constructed by building with

concrete blocks and then smoothing a fine-textured stucco over the surface, rounding the corners so the finished wall looks like adobe, and even capping the wall with natural stone.

Stucco is simply a mixture of cement, sand, a little lime, and water that can be smeared over surfaces. Sometimes coloring agents, such as powdered oxides available at paint stores, are added. Before coloring a whole batch of stucco, mix a small portion—about a number-10 can full (1–1.5 l)—carefully with a little powdered coloring, and then let it dry. The color lightens rather drastically as the surface dries. The best-looking colors for the garden are warm, natural ones that will set off the greens and intense

flower colors of plants—earthy beiges and muted ochers. Too much color in the stucco will be ostentatious and dominate the garden scene. The colors in the plants should dominate, so be judicious in your use of coloring agents. Just a light little hint will do it. If you know what you're going to plant by the wall, you can fine-tune the wall color to make a color harmony with it.

Cast concrete walls with steel reinforcing wire or rods in them should be built by professionals, especially if they are going to be higher than 3 feet (1 m). Many communities require building permits for such walls, and some building codes are positively baroque. Unless you are professionally familiar with the ins and outs of local codes and requirements, it's well worth the expense of hiring a licensed contractor to do the job. Not only that, but contractors can ordinarily get discounts on ready-made concrete delivered by truck in the quantities needed for cast concrete walls.

Hiring a contractor doesn't mean relinquishing your say about how the walls should look, where they go, what color they may be, and how they may be decorated.

One advantage of concrete walls is that they can curve and meander in smooth, tight, regular ways, making a nice contrast with the loose, natural forms of plants. A smooth concrete wall makes a simple, effective statement when it is dripping with sedum planted above it, or when ivy planted below it creeps up and softens its hard-edged lines.

Stuccoed over, a concrete-and-stone-rubble wall and a cast-concrete wall look about the same. Cast concrete is much stronger, however, and a very good choice for a retaining wall that holds a steep bank. The concrete-and-stone-rubble wall, with its differing materials that may or may not bond well together, is better used for separating areas, screening views, and decoration.

Walls themselves will decorate your garden, but you may choose to decorate your walls. The concrete for a cast wall may be loaded with aggregate—small round pebbles. If you remove the forms when the concrete has set stiff but is not yet completely hardened and solid, you may be able to take a steel brush to the surface and expose the rounded tops of the aggregate pebbles within. If these pebbles are of varied colors, the effect can be quite beautiful.

Consider topping your concrete wall with flat, broken shards of native stone set at an angle into the top of the poured

A plain-board fence in the Steele family backyard in Richmond, Virginia, is given the royal decorative treatment, and the result is sweetly charming. English ivy (Hedera helix) is grown up the fence to form living bunting, and wall sconces with Johnny-jump-ups (Viola tricolor) and a little bird feeder fill the spaces above the ivy. Below, other violas spatter dashes of color on the ground.

concrete while it is still wet. Or you may smooth the top of the poured concrete with a float and let it harden, then when the forms are removed, set the top with capstones that are just slightly broader than the wall. You can put mortar on the top of the wall and set the capstones on the wet mortar so that everything is sturdy when dry. Bricks can make a nice top to a concrete wall, too.

If you have access to beautiful tiles, especially those depicting flowers and garden scenes, consider setting them into the wall. Probably the easiest way to do this is to remove the form on the face side of the wall when the concrete is set but not completely hardened, chip out a spot for the tile, and then mortar it into the wall.

You can also paint your walls, with special concrete paints available for the purpose. Color applied while the stucco is still wet creates the time-honored look of fresco. Such techniques look best to my eye when done with restraint.

Brick Walls

People have been using bricks for walls for a good 5,000 years. The famous entrance gate to Nineveh, now in the Pergamon Museum in Berlin, is brick set with glazed figures of dragons and lions. The Israelites, you'll remember, made bricks for Pharaoh during their Egyptian captivity. Today, brick is still as popular as ever, and as beautiful as ever in the garden setting.

One of the prettiest garden sights I've ever seen was a brick wall with a yellow rose grown up onto it. The reddish brick color made a perfect visual harmony with the soft yellow roses, and the dark green foliage intensified the brick color and made a dark background for the roses.

If you plan to build a brick wall yourself, go to the library or bookstore and check out one of the how-to books on bricklaying. This is an ancient and rather complicated art, with plenty of jargon, that requires a good deal of practice before you become good at it. Don't assume that anyone with common sense and no experience can lay a brick wall. There really is much to know if it's to be done right, and if it isn't done right, the wall will soon become unstable and dangerous.

If the wall is to be more than 3 feet (1 m) tall, make sure you check to see if you need a building permit. Brick walls 3 or more feet tall need to be at least 8 inches (20 cm) wide — the width of two bricks and a channel of mortar between them. (Just as "2-by-4" lumber is not actually 2 inches by 4 inches, so most bricks are not 4 by 8 inches. The most commonly used bricks, called "nominal" bricks, are 7½ x 3½ x 2¼ inches, or 19.1 x 8.9 x 5.7 cm.)

Unlike dry stone walls, which will stay together just about forever even though they have no mortar, brick walls must be laid with mortar, because rainwater will penetrate completely through a brick wall with no mortar, and the individual bricks are light enough that winter freezing and thawing will push them around and soon knock the wall down. Brick walls also need poured concrete footers twice the width of the wall and 12 inches (.3 m) deep for walls over 2 or 3 feet (.6–1 m) high. The footer insures a sturdy base that is dead level in all directions. The mortar in a wall out of level soon disintegrates from internal

stresses, and once that happens, the wall disintegrates with it. Brick is so beautiful, however, that these caveats shouldn't discourage you from using it to decorate your garden.

To understand a description of a brick wall, you need to know the meaning of three terms: header, stretcher, and rowlock.

A header is a brick seen head-on in the wall. That is, you see the 3½-inch width and 2¼-inch height of the end of the brick. Its length reaches into the interior of the wall across two rows of bricks, just as a header or bind stone reaches across the courses of stone in a stone wall.

A stretcher is a brick seen lengthwise in a wall — that is, you see its length of 7½ inches and its height of 2¼ inches.

Rowlock construction is used on top of a brick wall to cap it. Bricks are set on

edge across the two rows of bricks underneath so that as you look at the wall you see a row of bricks 2¼ inches wide and 3½ inches deep. Brick walls can be constructed in a variety of patterns, but the most important and most frequently used patterns are also the strongest. These patterns are the common bond, running

---

This striking fence is an English wattle hurdle — and a very well made one at that. Young, pliable saplings of alder or osier are woven through the uprights and often have a small window woven in, which the English call a twilly hole, although this example has none. Young alder is planted in front of it and will overtake the hurdle within a few years, making a living fence. But by then the hurdle will have served its purpose and begun to disintegrate. This one was found at Snowshill Manor, Gloucestershire, England.

Opposite: *An interesting variation on the picket fence wends its way through Connie Cross's garden in Cutchogue, New York. The fence is a simple affair given rhythm by alternating the heights of the pickets. A collection of healthy-looking hostas anchors the fence to the ground.*

Below: *The traditional white picket fence at Mrs. Rabion's garden in Milwaukee provides a cheerful setting and a welcome bit of regularity for a bright group of busy perennials, including the featured orange blossoms of* Lilium *'Enchantment', with supporting roles played by bee balm (*Monarda didyma)*, *Lysimachia, and solidago.*

bond, English bond, and Flemish bond, and are variations of patterns of headers and stretchers (except for the running bond, which is entirely stretchers). Other patterns are certainly possible and sometimes used, but the aforementioned are the strongest bonds. Avoid bonds where joints are set one above another.

A series of staggered bricks in a wall, with open spaces between them, makes a screened effect, through which you can catch glimpses of sunlight and foliage beyond.

Gardens can be edged and raised beds defined by low brick walls two feet (.6 m) tall or less. For walls this size, you can use just one row of bricks set in a running bond. You'll still need to pour a 6-inch (15 cm) footer of concrete, however, or one winter's frosts will crack and heave the wall.

For taller walls, especially ones that will reach 6 feet (1.8 m), you'll need to use steel reinforcing rods driven down into the wet mortar between two courses of brick, and then construct pilasters, or

piers, of bricks that are locked into the wall by overlapping bonds every 12 feet (3.7 m) down the length of the wall. If this seems excessive, it isn't. These rules have been created by bricklayers over the centuries who want to get the job done, but also want to get it done right. They know that without reinforcement and pilasters, tall brick walls are subject to earth movements that will soon enough crack the mortar, after which it falls out and after which the wall collapses.

Serpentine walls that curve this way and that are sturdier than straight brick walls. They are good for edging raised beds and herb gardens and for edging curved pathways. Brick walls can tie the wild garden to the house by starting at the back door and extending out into the shrubs and flowers of the planted garden.

Bricks can be used to build retaining walls and for terracing, but because they must hold heavy soil, they need extra-strong footers and several layers of brick reinforced solidly with steel rods. A good bond for this kind of wall is called by bricklayers a rowlock bond—stretchers alternate with headers along the row, but all bricks are set up on their sides. This leaves a 3-inch (7.6 cm) space between the stretchers, which can be filled with concrete and steel reinforcing rods.

It was a custom in England a couple of centuries ago to terrace the lawn around a manor house as it sloped down and away. The retaining brick wall, invisible from above, was called a ha-ha. It terraced the slope and kept the cows down in the lower pasture, because they couldn't climb

the wall. The visual effect from the house was of lawn running seamlessly out to the hedgerows or woods, and cattle grazing rustically around the estate.

▣ A "Natural" Wall That Includes Planting Spaces

What do we mean by a "natural" wall? A wall built by a human being for human purposes is the product of planning. Mother Nature throws up walls, too, or rather excavates them, without previous planning. We find these natural walls in places where rushing water has carried away soil and sand and sediment and left only stones large and small, jumbled together on the slopes. These jumbles often have their own form of stability, because the rocks are jammed together in ways that have kept them in place, the unstable ones having tumbled down long ago.

Such water-washed slopes are very instructive. If you find a gully where winter and spring freshets tend to torrent down the hillside, you'll find the exposed rocks that make a natural wall.

The first thing you'll notice about this wall is that it isn't a stack of stones, one above the other. That arrangement is a human concept. Nature's wall is the result of another concept altogether—or actually a whole web of interdependent concepts, including weather patterns, geological spoil banks, hydrological and gravitational effects, and so on. The end result is a slope of stones that holds in the soil behind it, the fortuitous result of nature's action.

Because the stones aren't stacked according to a human plan, there's a hap-hazard quality to their construction. Big stones are interspersed with small ones, and the stacking tends to be staggered tiers. There are spaces between the stones in front and the ones slightly higher behind them. The rushing water has carried soil into these crevices, and the seeds of plants have lodged in the soil. Now the bank is composed of stones, ferns, wild columbines, mosses, and other wildings.

What a marvelous idea for a wall in our own garden! I have made many such walls since I first noticed how nature constructs hers, and they are always satisfying and natural-looking and afford wonderful planting places for alpines and other small plants that will grow in the soil-packed crevices between the rocks.

I begin at the lowest ground level and sink several large rocks almost entirely into the earth, so just their tops—never more than their top third—are showing. Around and behind these, I sink smaller stones, some horizontally, some positioned vertically. Every stone is buried at least halfway into the soil. I use a variety of sizes and try to make sure the stones are all of the same composition and color. Working back and up the bank, I insert the largest stones first, then the medium-size ones around them, then the smallest stones in the spaces where stones join each other.

The end result is a natural-looking tiered stone embankment, with lots of little shelves and ledges with soil in them. I plant succulents, California poppies, species tulips, verbena, alyssum, and other drought-tolerant plants in these spaces.

Decorative Fencing

Wood Paneling

A paneled wood fence, with upright boards close together so you can't see through, provides the greatest visual security for your property. Such a fence also makes a fine backdrop for espaliered trees and a support for vines (see page 179).

In most areas, a building permit will be required for fences over 5 feet tall—and a wood-paneled fence should be at least 6 to 7 feet (1.8–2.1 m). You may decide to build it 5 feet tall and then attach 2-foot-high sections of prefabricated framed latticework on top. In some areas, doing so will obviate the need for a permit and give you a place to tie vines.

The wood, even after several seasons of rains and sun cause it to turn silver, provides a natural color for the plants placed in front of it. If you do decide to paint it, you may find that a dark stain and preservative is preferable to whitewash or light paint. The dark color makes a great backdrop for featured plants, while a light fence will wash out subtle colors and compete for attention with your ornamental plantings.

A paneled fence forms a dead stop for the eye, which makes it useful as a positive visual screen against ugly neighboring yards or buildings or views you'd rather not see. Remember, however, that used along a property line and viewed from a street or sidewalk, such a fence looks rather foreboding and unfriendly, and tempts passersby to find a chink or knothole to peer through, just to see what's going on.

Wattle

Few gardeners decorate their gardens with wattle fencing anymore—and that's too bad. These fences can be very attractive, and they use local materials that usually grow in bogs and marshy areas that need periodic cleaning anyway.

Think of a wattle fence as a big screen, woven like a basket, using flexible twigs. When a section of wattle fencing is finished, it can be left in place or moved elsewhere in the garden, making it very handy to have around (see pages 179–80).

These fences are very decorative and make good boundaries between patios and the garden proper. Plant them in the ornamental garden with sweet peas or morning glories, or in the vegetable garden with edible peas.

Split-rail Fencing

Split-rail fences have an 18th- or 19th-century look to them, especially when set up as a zigzag fence. This was common in the days when there was lots of easily split old-growth timber, and plenty of room to set the fence up—zigzag split-rail fences take up a great deal of space.

Split rails can also be used with upright posts through which holes have been drilled, and such posts are usually found at building supply and garden centers. Using posts with holes, the ends of split-rail fences can be inserted in the holes and a straight run of fence put up.

These fences have a rustic appeal,

aren't usually higher than 3 or 4 feet (1–1.2 m), and are fine for directing traffic, growing vines such as grapes or clematis, and separating a kept part of the property from the wilder, woodsy portion in the background. They don't give much visual screen, but zigzags are good at fencing out cattle. When the split rails are used with drilled-out posts, dogs and other animals can go right under them.

▣ Picket Fencing

Picket fences offer the garden decorator the most choices for creating pretty visual effects. These fences are light and airy, yet sturdy enough to keep out animals and unwanted human traffic. They are friendly and pretty along a street or sidewalk, and have a Victorian or even colonial look to them that's always pleasant.

Picket fences are usually painted white, making them a perfect foil for the dark green leaves and bright colors of roses.

Most picket fencing available in building-supply stores has rather wide pickets, usually all of the same length, and with pointed pickets at the top. It's not hard to make your own, however, from

Latticework, especially when painted white, gives one of the most sought-after effects in the garden—class. It echoes the formal retreats of the wealthy at the end of the Victorian age, and yet is simple and inexpensive to erect. This example of a latticework partition decorates Butchart Gardens in Victoria, British Columbia. It's overtopped with pelargoniums, with penstemons and petunias below.

relatively inexpensive 1-by-3 wood from the lumberyard, and this size gives an ideal look to the fence (see pages 180–81).

The Portland Garden Club in Portland, Oregon, erected this fence in front of a stand of large timber bamboo. It's a clever and very decorative piece of work, as the open slats in the fence repeat the effect of the tall bamboo canes behind them. The foot of the fence is softened with shaggy mounds of foliage.

Hall in Derbyshire, a very finely wrought work with elaborate twists and arabesques that would steal the show in any garden. Other notable wrought-iron works from a slightly earlier time are the fences and gates of Jean Tijou done for William and Mary at Hampton Court Palace.

In the United States, stop by Dumbarton Oaks in Washington, D.C., where master garden designer Beatrix Farrand turned a farm into a series of lovely spaces and gardens, with reflecting pools, gorgeous walls, and exciting decorations that will give you many ideas for your own property—and some extra-fine wrought-iron fence and balustrade work.

While much wrought iron is done in abstract curlicues and arabesques alternating with straight lines, some of the most beautiful is done in patterns of leaves and branches. These pieces are exceptionally flattering in the garden, as they echo the shapes and patterns of the leaves and branches around them, and when the sun shines through, they throw lovely, natural patterns on the ground around them.

Because wrought-iron fencing is so ornamental, it's best not cluttered over with vines and plantings—although a rose trailing on a wrought-iron fence

◉ Latticework

About all you need to construct for a latticework fence is the posts and rails, for latticework comes ready-made in various lengths and heights.

Check your local building-supply store for the sizes they stock, then set your posts and fix your rails to accommodate that size of framed-in latticework. Use 1-by-1 wood strips nailed on both sides of the framed latticework to hold it firmly in place. Nail in one side first, set in your framed lattice, then nail in the open side.

Painted latticework looks nice— especially when the paint color is coordinated with the plants growing on it. I recently saw a cup-and-saucer vine (*Cobaea scandens*) growing on a lattice frame painted robin's-egg blue, and the effect was enormously charming. The cobaea's deep purple cups were made even prettier by the cheery blue-green of the paint behind it.

◉ Wrought Iron and Wire

Wrought iron—that ironwork which is heated to red or white hot and hammered into shape by a leather-aproned smith— is a beautiful material in its own right, even before it's placed in the garden.

In the garden, it provides security but allows one to see through it. This feature makes it perfect when used within a property, where privacy is insured, but a fence is needed, either for animal control, for visual appeal, or to direct foot traffic.

Wrought-iron fencing—and even buildings—had a vogue in Victorian times, and throughout Europe you can still see many beautiful examples of ironwork. A notable example is an 18th-century fence by Robert Bakewell at Melbourne

can make a pretty picture. Let the fence be its own feature, and use wrought iron where people can see it—along walkways above patios, and along sidewalks where you won't mind passersby seeing into the property—and where, in fact, you'd like them to see the gardens you've created.

◙ Other Ideas for Fencing

Ideas for fencing are limited only by our imaginations. I've seen a fence made of two rows of round posts about 12 inches apart, alternated so they form a zigzag line, with 6 inches of open space between the posts. It's all verticals, but effectively provides a barrier to humans and large animals with no horizontal railings.

Rustic fences can be made of posts and pole railings, with skinned poles set X-fashion into the rectangles formed by the railings and posts. The Victorians used to plant a row of fruit-tree saplings about 3 feet (1 m) apart and, when the saplings were about 4 inches (10 cm) in diameter, trim off all low branches and nail or lash railings to the trunks, making a living fence that also bore fruit.

....

Don't ever throw away broken china. Mr. and Mrs. Malcolm Buckenham of Brimscombe, Gloucestershire, England, saved theirs and had enough Wedgwood china to cover a wall that flanks a set of oft-repaired steps. The use of the rangy dianthus, with its blue-green leaves and pink flowers against the broken dinnerware, is inspired. And lest there be too much cool blue, the scene is warmed by the variegated leaves on either side of the dianthus.

You can stagger the length of uprights set between posts and railings so they make a rhythmic pattern, like the rise and fall of notes played by a jazz musician. Bamboo can be woven into screens that attach to uprights and can be removed for winter storage. Long poles can be set into the ground at 45-degree angles, and then another row of poles set opposite them at 45-degree angles, with the two sets lashed together to make a diagonal trellis fence.

If you're looking for ideas for fencing, keep a notebook in your car and make a sketch of interesting fences you see as you travel around. You'll soon have pages full and plenty to choose from.

Beautiful Gates

◻ Interesting Designs

For a formal gate, not much beats wrought iron. Set into a solid wall, it allows the visitor a glimpse of what's inside, without revealing all. While the wall may be impenetrable, the gate is open and airy.

The wrought iron can be worked into arabesques or simply be formed and hammered into regular patterns such as vertical or horizontal bars or cross-hatched diamonds. In their most formal incarnations, such gates are taller than a man— usually tall enough for a carriage—and have a top piece, called an overthrow, spanning the area above the gate and highly ornamented. Jean Tijou was seminal here and influenced many on the

Continent and in England to create highly ornamented gates and overthrows. Tijou himself specialized in repoussé— the technique of hammering hot metal from the back to raise a design on the front. He used to create the repoussé and then have blacksmiths heat the iron and forge two sides together, making hollow three-dimensional designs.

Wrought-iron gates have another advantage over wooden gates: they won't sag and bend out of shape. When you build or install a wooden gate, it's very important that the gate be as light as possible, with more bracing, larger hinges, and more firmly set gateposts than you would ordinarily imagine it needs. With

gates, overbuilding is not unwarranted. Over time, the weight of the gate swaying on the hinges will cause the bottom of the gate to drag on the ground. The gate then looks off-square and mars the beauty of the garden (see page 181).

◻ Incorporating Arches into the Gateway

When you overtop a gate with an arch, vines and climbers grown up on the arch will spill down and surround you with beauty and fragrance each time you walk through.

Prefabricated arches come in a variety of styles and materials. Wooden gate arches often have

Above: *The wrought-iron gate to the Bourton House garden at Bourton-on-the-Hill, Gloucestershire, England, is a grand example of classic English style, recalling an entire cultural history in its delicately figured points and swirls. The countryside beyond the gate is just as classically English. Note that each square of the deliciously designed pavement has a different motif.*

Opposite: *The brick pathway below has its curves echoed in the design on the wooden gate, the curving top of the gate itself, and the luscious bower of sweetheart roses (Rosa 'Cécile Brunner') that overtops it all. Ivy and twining stems of powerfully fragrant star jasmine (Trachelospermum jasminoides) join the roses in climbing the bower's supports here at Jody Honnen's garden in Rancho Santa Fe, California.*

latticework sides and slatted tops, which make it easy to attach twining vines. Wrought-iron and steel arches are also commonly found, usually painted black. Steel arches may be painted green and overgrown with roses, causing the steel framework to disappear.

If you already have a gate, the arch should match it. If you have yet to construct your gate, check the arbors available at your garden center and build a gate that matches the style of the arbor you choose (see page 182).

Some of the more popular archways for gates have seating incorporated along their sides—although I don't think I've ever seen anyone sitting in them. But it's nice to think that the gateway to or from a part of the garden gives the visitor a place to sit and rest before moving on.

Arches have to be firmly secured if they are to carry the weight of climbing vines. The vines may not weigh much when they are out of leaf in winter, but when in full leaf and flower, the plant material aloft can be quite heavy, and an unsecured archway will tumble over in a strong wind.

◉ Plants for Gateways

Climbing roses, of course, are the standard plant for an arched gateway. A 'Climbing Cecile Brunner', the "sweetheart rose," is a traditional one for this purpose; it has small pink flowers with a sweet little scent. Many favorite hybrid tea roses come in climbing form—for instance, there's 'Climbing Iceberg', 'Climbing Peace',

and 'Climbing Chrysler Imperial', among hundreds of others.

But if you want a rose that's dramatic and dramatically fragrant, try 'Don Juan'. It has a climbing habit to cover an archway, a deep rich red color, a pretty form, and a strong fragrance. Another fine rose for a semishady spot is the deep pink climbing bourbon rose, 'Zéphirine Drouhin'. In addition to being shade tolerant, it is very fragrant and has thornless canes.

While these suggestions are good ones, you should choose a rose that suits you. Study the catalogs or visit a rose garden and find a rose that impresses. There are thousands in cultivation.

Some of my favorite plants to grow up on arches above gateways are annuals like the cup-and-saucer vine (*Cobaea scandens*), sweet peas, morning glories for the morning, and moonflowers for the evening.

Among perennials, the finest of all for the warmer zones in my opinion is *Clematis montana* var. *rubens*, a stunningly beautiful vine that covers itself with four-petaled pink flowers in spring. In the colder zones, choose your favorite large-flowered clematis. The 'Comtesse de Bouchaud' is a rich pink variety that's heart-stoppingly beautiful. Grow it up one side of the arch and grow the fragrant white-to-blush-pink rambler 'New Dawn' up the other side, for an exquisite pairing. Or try deep purple-violet clematis 'Niobe' with 'New Dawn'.

Be creative. Run a grape, such as the seedless Concord-type 'Canadice', over the archway so you can pick fruit as you pass through. Espalier semidwarf apple trees up and over the top from both sides. Or grow *Passiflora edulis*—the edible passion fruit vine—over the archway. Perennial pea *(Lathyrus latifolius)* and Spanish jasmine *(Jasminum grandiflorum)* are also excellent choices for an archway.

Besides the standard archway over the gate, which may be just a couple of feet deep, you may decide to go for something more elaborate that may take a carpenter to build, such as an arched latticework passageway leading up to the gate, on which you can grow roses, some of the larger clematis such as *Clematis paniculata*, or the well-behaved *Wisteria venusta*, which will drape its blue-purple flowers down through the arching latticework.

A passageway leading to a gate can also be formed from huge wrought-iron wickets welded together, an arrangement that can then be planted with golden-chain trees *(Laburnum watereri)* tied over its arches.

....

Opposite: *Trumpet vine* (Campsis radicans) *billows and leaps from the top of this latticework archway over a gate at Jim Smith's garden in Columbia, South Carolina. Notice that the archway has seats built into either side. The vine will need a good trimming after this season, as it is a very vigorous grower that will soon swallow up the structure.*

Right: *An arched gateway in Genie White's garden in Charlotte, North Carolina, turns a very simple fence into a spot of extraordinary beauty. Notice that the fence is faced with wire mesh small enough to keep out rabbits and domestic animals. The creamy white rose is 'Trier', and it is delightfully fragrant, while the pink climber is 'Bubble Bath'. The wire mesh over the top of the arch prevents the roses from growing through the supports down into the walkway, and the brick path adds a gracious touch of formality.*

CHAPTER FOUR

Paths and Walkways

In the bang-bang, hurry-up world in which we spend far too much time, a road, path, or walkway must take us somewhere. It's the destination that's important, and the sooner we get there, the better. In a garden, however, where time runs at a natural pace, the path and walkway are not so much the means to a destination as a destination themselves. They are the way we wander as we enjoy the garden from many angles, in different aspects, in morning and evening, through all the seasons. We need to contruct paths and walkways that are enjoyable as places, rather than just as corridors for movement to somewhere else.

The best place to put a path is where a path already exists. Notice how the children go through the property, or where the dog runs, or the route you usually take as you go from one place to another. If there's already a path—even if it's only a route where the grass or weeds are more trampled than elsewhere—construct your path there.

We've all seen shopping malls and institutional places where shrubbery was installed with no regard to how people want to move, but only with a thought to how people should move. The shrubbery usually has holes worn in it where people push their way through it to go the way they want. Trying to defeat an existing path is just plain contrary and wrong-headed. Make things easy for people, but don't let them see all of your path at once. Let the path reveal the treasures of the garden piecemeal.

It's fun when paths offer people choices. Which way do you go when an unfamiliar path forks in front of you as you wander it? The decision could affect every subsequent thing you do, or place you encounter, in that garden. When you choose one route, there's always a part of your mind that wonders what was down the other one. It may remind you of life's choices. Early in life, each little choice has monumental consequences for the rest of your days. Later in life, when your decisions have branched and rebranched many times, only monumental decisions usually provoke great consequences. Twists and turns lengthen the path as well, prolonging the fun of exploring the garden or viewing its current state. The more the path meanders, the slower the visitor must walk and the more probability that he or she will notice some of the joys you have planted along the way.

Although a path is seemingly a thing of dead stone or brick, life is there. Summer's plants spill out upon it as if gushing their enthusiasm for life. A bird can stand in the middle of a path with some certainty that a cat won't be able to reach it before it can fly away. In moist and shady places, the smothering moss will come to cover up the bricks. In late fall a path may fill with browned leaves, and a band of sparrows may flit and dart into the sticks of the bare bushes as you pass by. In winter sunbeams will prism in the snowbanks, and the flash of a cardinal's color will promise the future season's verbenas. It won't be long then before spring's first modest pleasures will seem like sumptuous delights.

Of course, the very construction of the path offers you a chance to express yourself. Gardens—plants, paths, walls, stones, and all—are like poems when they are well designed. The path will seem totally natural, and each step along it will feel satisfying, as though it's giving footing to your wandering whims. If it went any other way, it would be forced and awkward. Eastern philosophy describes the perfect way as heaven's way—the Dharma. A way is, after all, a path. More than any other feature that decorates your garden, the path can be most evocative of poetic perfection if it follows heaven's way. And how do we know heaven's way? We've been told that heaven's kingdom is within us.

The Japanese envision the garden path as symbolic of life's journey, returning one to the place where one started so

long ago. Thus the path tells a story in its wanderings through the garden world. Think of that, and of the story you'd like to tell, as you plan and build the ways that take you through the garden.

 ## Pretty Paths

◉ Path Materials

When considering which materials you might use to make a path, first consider where you are in the garden and what you want to have happen there. If your path is leading you down between two gorgeously planted borders of perennials, you don't want the visual impact of the path to compete with the flower beds, and so something subdued, regular, and easy to walk on without having to glance down at is

Left: *A poetic expression of a path is created at Fred Watson's garden in Alstead, New Hampshire, where large boulders with a flat surface are set into the emerald carpet of the lawn. One large, rough stone protrudes above the plane of the others, as if to be a perch, or perhaps an obstacle to be skirted.*

Page 74: *A flagstone walkway has been inlaid with living emerald lines of mondo grass (Ophiopogon japonicus) in Sharon Abroms's garden in Atlanta. This very striking design strongly pulls the eye through the gateway to the focal point— the terra-cotta pot in the distance. The effect is to lure the visitor through the gate to explore the next passage.*

called for—brick, for instance. You would not want a path of lumpy stones, tricky steps, or slippery rocks that require the visitor to look down to make sure he or she is not going to slip or stumble.

Nor should you use material that is too bright, such as white crushed-quartz gravel, which generates dazzling color and reflected light from the path that overwhelm the borders. You must let the stars of the scene shine.

◉ Concrete with Pebbles

Dark, rounded pebbles, the kind dug from a beach or riverbed, set into concrete make the finest all-purpose path material (see pages 182–83). The pebbles are pretty; they glisten when wet and yet are not slippery; they are dark and don't interfere with the plantings; they are permanent, they allow no weed growth and the path is never muddy; and they are widely available at building-material yards.

◎ Stone Blocks and Flagstones

A very effective and decorative look is achieved by using flat blocks or pieces of stone in open geometric patterns, with gravel set into the openings. You can also use stone blocks to edge a path of concrete with pebbles, or a path made of gravel with no concrete.

Here we broach the subject of gravel paths, where gravel is simply laid on a pathway of soil. This is commonly done, but be aware that the gravel tends to spill off the path, and weeds can easily grow through the gravel—so a gravel path takes less initial work but more maintenance. Don't use more than an inch (2.5 cm) of gravel, or the footing may become difficult as gravel chips slide against one another. The gravel will need to be renewed from time to time.

If you plan to use flagstones or fieldstones set into the earth with no concrete or mortar, underlay them with an inch of sand for drainage, which will help keep the stones in place during winter freezes and thaws. Where there's adobe clay soil, set the stones in the clay when it's wet and workable, and when the clay dries, it will be almost as durable as cement.

In a sinuous walkway in Ginger Epstein's garden in Atlanta, cement prevents loose pebbles from being ground into the subsoil or kicked off into the surrounding plantings, while the ferns, azaleas, and mondo grass (Ophiopogon japonicus) will not be able to invade.

Bury the flagstones or fieldstones so their flattest, best sides are just a bit above ground level. Fit the stones together as closely as possible, but here and there leave some gaps of a few inches, and in them plant low-growing flowering plants like woolly thyme, mother-of-thyme, alyssum, and iberis. Grass, too, can be planted or allowed to grow between stones in a path. If the stones are set flat into the ground, you can run the lawnmower over the grass to keep it looking neat.

In formal gardens, use geometric designs in the path, or use the formal simplicity of pebbles set in concrete. In woodsy gardens or less formal settings, use stones set into the earth, cobbled paths, stones set on edge, and naturalistic arrangements of stone.

The designs you choose are limited only by your imagination. Keep an eye out for inspiration by making notes about fine stonework where you find it. Use that notebook you keep in the car to sketch a design you find particularly appealing.

Most often, the look, color, and size of the stones you're working with will suggest a design, and those suggestions, if well followed, tend to be the most satisfying.

▣ Colored Concrete and Mosaics

Of course, you can just pour slabs of concrete to make a walkway, but plain concrete walks tend to look institutional. How much better it is to decorate the concrete. One friend of mine experimented with coloring concrete and cement in

walkways, with fine results. He used muriatic acid—a weak solution of hydrochloric acid used to clean surfaces—on the cement. (You'll of course remember from your high-school chemistry that cement is mostly calcium carbonate and rather alkaline, while hydrochloric acid is a strong acid that will easily react with the calcium carbonate to form calcium chloride, carbon dioxide, and water.) When muriatic acid is applied to cement, the carbon dioxide fizzes off as a gas, and the calcium chloride dissolves in the water. Into this liquid can be poured variously colored solutions of permanent dyes, stains, powdered pigments, and so on. As the prepared and colored surfaces dry, the color becomes chemically bonded into the cement. When colors are subtle and earthy and used with discretion, the effect can be quite beautiful. You should experiment with coloring agents and small squares of cement that you pour as test samples to make sure you're getting what you want before you color a walk-

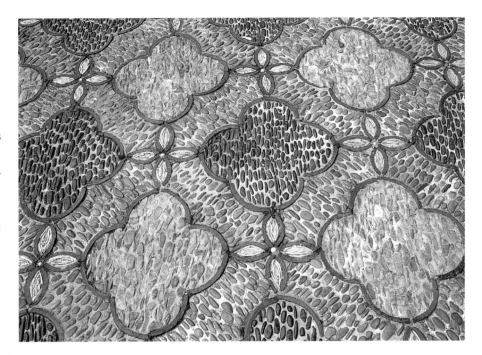

Right: *This astounding detail is found in a walkway at the Dr. Sun Yat-Sen Classical Chinese Garden in Vancouver, British Columbia. It's such a pretty and decorative idea that it makes one jealous of the person who has the time to carefully create such a pleasant picture in stone.*

Opposite: *The gravel path at Mrs. W. Irving's garden at Greencroft House, Great Strickland, England, gives a neat appearance. Although the gravel— called "chippings" in England—is loose, it's perfectly maintained to be weed free and to stay within its boundaries.* Saxifrages, Geranium cinereum, *and* Iris subcaulescens *decorate the pathway.*

way. My friend used the technique with stencils to create borders and edging along his walkway.

An acquaintance in California has developed one of the more interesting techniques for using concrete in the garden path. He digs out a bowl-shaped depression about the size of a large stone in the soil and smooths the sides, then fills it with concrete. When it has firmed up, but is not completely hardened, he pries it out of the soil, turns it over so its flat side is down, wets the surface, and sprinkles it with a mixture of sand and cement with a little earth- or stone-colored dry pigment such as you can buy at a paint store. He drizzles it gently with a fine spray, then lets it harden. When made properly, these handmade stones look very natural and serve as stepping stones or pathway pavers.

Wet cement pathways will accept all kinds of decorative objects to enhance their appearance or lend a touch of humor. Bits of broken crockery, glass, mirror, colored pebbles, marbles, and other bits of bric-a-brac can be set into wet cement to dress up a pathway. Just make sure that what you use won't rust and discolor.

The Romans, and the Byzantines after them, were masters of mosaic work, in which small tesserae—bits of colored tiles—would be set into wet plaster to create stunning pictures. It's still possible to purchase tesserae in various colors, and while it's an ambitious project and not for every garden setting, a mosaic pathway can be unforgettable. It's a technique much more frequently seen in Europe than the United States, but it's always very decorative and effective.

Bricks are laid in a decorative herringbone pattern at Ellen Coster's garden in Cutchogue, New York. Not only does this design produce a very ornamental pattern on the garden floor, but the interlocking bricks give the pattern strength and stability. The herringbone bricks are nicely accented by the diagonal design in the latticework fence.

Concrete blocks can be set on their sides and sunk to their tops into the soil to provide a firm base for driving a vehicle up to the garden, while the empty spaces in the blocks and the areas between the blocks are filled with topsoil into which grass is sown. Many preformed concrete blocks have interior designs and look pretty, but even ordinary cinderblock, turned on its side and sunk to the top into the soil, will do the job. There are even cement blocks made especially for this purpose; called turf blocks, they are widely available at building-supply shops.

The function of the blocks is to give rigidity to the soil so that even in rainy weather you can drive a vehicle on it. The grass that grows in the soil-filled spaces can be cut as usual with the lawnmower, since the blocks are buried to their faces. Seen from the side, or from any distance, the concrete blocks are not very noticeable, and the area will look like a swath of grass, but it will hold firmly. Punctured steel sheets are also available for this purpose, but they are expensive and don't look as good as turf block.

◉ Brick Walkways

Up until now, we've been discussing path materials that are relatively diffi-cult to work with—stones and poured concrete. But brick walkways have all the advantage.

First, they are beautiful. A pathway of warm, earth-colored, dull red brick perfectly sets off the green foliage and floral colors beside it. Old brick is even more beautiful than new brick, because old brick acquires a patina and mottling with age that makes it a joy to work with in the garden. If you can locate a supply of old bricks, even with chunks of mortar still attached, snap them up.

I once ran across a truckload of these bricks, which had been part of a bricked street in Philadelphia. Years of traffic had worn the edges of the bricks smooth and round. I made a patio and pathway in front of the house from them that looked from the moment I finished it as though it had been there for a century. These bricks had mortar attached, and yes, it was tedious and time-consuming work gently chipping off the mortar with a chisel and hammer, but with the radio tuned to sports or music, and with the fine day slowly rolling over me, it was a calming task in fine contrast to the usual helter-skelter of my days.

I learned some tips doing this: soak the bricks overnight in water before you chip them, as wet mortar comes loose more easily than dry. Finish the job with a steel brush. Don't try to get every bit of mortar off the sides. Chisel the mortar gently, as hard raps tend to break old bricks. Handle an old brick with care, setting it gently aside when you're finished with it.

If you have no old bricks, building material yards sell bricks made to look old.

You'll find they sell all kinds of bricks in varying colors, patterns, sizes, and shapes. Don't think you have to limit yourself to standard burnt-red brick. Use several kinds in interesting patterns in your walkway. For instance, basketweave square patterns of ordinary red brick can be separated by slender bricks of ocher or whitish mauve, set on their sides. The walkway can then be edged with bricks set in a rowlock pattern. You might consider excavating the side edging a half-inch deeper than the path surface so that rainwater runs onto the brick edging before flowing away.

While paving brick comes in an almost infinite variety of shapes and colors, good old-fashioned red brick still suits the garden best for an all-purpose path. Make sure your brick is rated for severe weather, and construct the body of the path by excavating soil about 4 inches (10 cm) deep, spreading about 1¼ inches (3.2 cm) of sand on the smooth, level soil, then setting your bricks—finishing the job by sweeping fine sand into the joints between bricks. This arrangement allows for good drainage in the winter and for

Although this interesting pathway is located in Solano Beach, California, in the Gronborg family garden, its mixture of gray and red brick edged with water-smoothed river or beach cobbles is an idea that would work anywhere. Notice that the walk reverts to a stone path a little farther on, proving again that variety is the spice not only of life, but of the garden as well. Alstroemeria's strawberry pink flowers and hot-colored canna edge the path at left.

struction, we use the slightly smaller nominal brick, which leaves room for mortared joints. Nominal bricks aren't modular—that is, the width of two bricks doesn't equal one brick's length.) When buying brick, set two bricks side by side and then check to see if they equal one brick length. If they are nominal bricks, the length will be a half inch longer than two widths. If you try to do an interlocking pattern with nominal bricks, you'll be coming up a half inch short with every two bricks.

The most common interlocking pattern is the basketweave. Two bricks are laid vertically side by side, then two are laid horizontally, then two vertically, then two horizontally, and so forth across the width of the path. The next course begins with two horizontals below the top course's first two verticals, and so forth to the end of the row.

A herringbone pattern is common in brick walks, and it is one of the most attractive and stable patterns. The same running-bond pattern that works to stabilize a wall also stabilizes a walkway. What doesn't work well is a stacked pattern of rows of bricks directly over each other. There's no interlock with this pattern, so it's weak.

One of the advantages of brick is that it is an easy material to handle, and being modular, can be set in straight or curved patterns. To make a curved brick path, define the path space by laying a garden hose along one curved edge, then excavate a shovelful of soil along that line. Now move the hose to what will be the other side of the path and lay it down in a line parallel to the first one, keeping the distance between the lines equal by using a measuring stick as you go. Now excavate a shovelful of soil along the second line, then excavate the soil from the entire path bed.

When the path is excavated and sand laid level and smooth in the bottom, put in your bricks entirely along one side first. A running bond of stretchers set lengthwise in the path's direction will have a "fast" look as the eye is carried along the bricks. If the bricks are set crossways across the path, the visual effect will be much slower. Start the bricks and run the first course down the path. Bricks are small enough that the minuscule triangular gaps formed between them as you follow the curve will be hardly noticeable. Then set in your second course against the first and so on until you reach the other side. That way, if there are any awkward places where you need to cut a brick to fill in, it will be at the side of the path and not out in the middle. Then set in your second line of edgers.

It's important to set in a row of edging bricks to stabilize the edges of the pathway, or the path-paving bricks will split off and work loose, and gaps will open in the

expansion and contraction during freezes and thaws. You will have a path that lasts for many, many years. Don't be tempted to set the bricks on the bare soil, or freezes and thaws will kick them out and rumple their surface. Avoid mortared brick pathways, as these are difficult to construct, prone to weathering, and don't function as well as sand-set brick paths.

Choose an interlocking pattern, and make sure your bricks are true-sized bricks of 2¾ by 4 by 8 inches. (For wall con-

remaining brickwork. These edging bricks can be set in as rowlocks (bricks set horizontally on their edges), stretchers (bricks set horizontally on their faces), soldiers (bricks set upright with their wide faces looking down the pathway), sailors (bricks set upright with their wide faces looking toward the other side of the path), or a dog-tooth design (bricks set into the ground at an angle so a triangular edge juts above the surface). An edging of poured concrete or large stone ashlars, however, is sturdier and proof against wandering pathway bricks. (An ashlar is a rectangular piece of cut stone.) A 6-by-6-by-18-inch ashlar of gray stone (15 x 15 x 46 cm) would be the perfect edger for a brick path and will probably look the best, too.

Garden centers often sell terra-cotta tiles, including tiles with ropework tops, for edging paths. These can make a beau-

....

Opposite: *Squares of slats nailed to frames are placed this way and that to make a quick-draining, sure-footed path into a place where stone is an even greater feature than the plants. In the foreground are flat flagstones, large and small cobbles, and a gravel surface that leads back to a gravel berm with plantings that resemble dolphins. A provocative menhir makes a vertical statement. This is Sonja Gauron's garden at Le Perray en Yvelines, France.*

Right: *In another part of Sonja Gauron's garden a striking design takes the eye off the plantings and pulls it swiftly down the diamond pathway to the firebrick and gravel circles set with unadorned, thrown terra-cotta pots. Here the emphasis is on the ingenuity of the human decorative elements rather than the deftness of plant combinations and their colors and shapes.*

tiful and decorative edging that keeps bricks in place.

Sometimes plants make good edgers. Although not as stable as stone or brick edging, closely spaced dwarf box or other low-growing woody plants like rosemary, clipped back and forming tight masses of roots, will help stabilize bricks and path materials.

Railroad ties or sturdy 4-by-4s cut from rot-resistant wood such as black locust also make good edging, and the contrast of brick and wood is a visual treat. The wood will eventually rot away, but this may take many years.

◙ Tile Paths

It's really quite entertaining to visit a building-materials yard and look over the tiles and pavers available these days. You'll find just about any shape and color you can imagine—and quite a few that you can't. Before you rush out to see what your supplier has, first consider fitting the tile to the garden. Generally speaking, quarry tile is more suitable for more elegant and refined formal types of English or French gardens, while patio tiles are best in Spanish, Italian, Mexican, tropical, southwestern, or California-style gardens.

Large, earth-colored Mexican patio tiles are made of widely available hard-fired clay that acquires red, ocher, or buff coloring. Glazed kinds are available for interior paving and are sometimes used outdoors, but their glazed surfaces become slick during wet weather. Mexican patio tiles are commonly found in 12-by-12,

6-by-12, and 6-by-6 sizes and look beautiful in a southwestern or Californian garden of succulents and cacti. As a paving for pathways, they are gorgeous as their warm, earthy colors mix well with many garden flowers, especially those that give a tropical or western look, such as gaillardia, fatsia, California poppy, yucca, and sempervivums.

A finer grade of tile is called quarry tile and is more expensive—and elegant—than rustic Mexican tiles. Colors range from blue-gray to gray to brick. Like Mexican tiles, quarry tiles are usually an inch or less thick, and have roughened surfaces for outdoor use and even corrugations for use where wet conditions prevail.

Both types of tile are very hard and impervious to water, but need a firm underpinning. It may seem like a lot of work, but the ideal underpinning is a slab of poured concrete down the length of the path. For an elegant and very decorative path leading from a patio area or the house into the garden, tiles are hard to beat. In the garden, less expensive materials can be used.

An assemblage of stones creates a rich tapestry of textures in Fred Watson's garden in Alstead, New Hampshire. Large, light gray ashlars are set into the ground at right angles and millstones are set between them. Variously colored and shaped smaller stones are used to fill the spaces. The edges of this tapestry are set with stones that create planting spaces for small shrubs like the evergreen mounds and the yellow-flowered Potentilla fruticosa.

▣ Mixed Media

One of the most decorative strategies of all for garden paths is the use of mixed media. One can set flagstones in the path and surround them with pebbled concrete. Flat stones can be set edgewise into the soil to form patterns, and cobbles set into the pattern's open spaces. Tiles and bricks can be mixed. Stones, tiles, bricks, pebbles, cobbles, setts (rectangular blocks of granite or sandstone used for paving), glass, metal—anything durable, actually, will help give a path diversity and interest.

The question becomes, then, how much interest do we want our paths to have? If they look like a circus, they could detract from the gardens. Suffice it to say that mixing media in the path can be a fascinating way to enliven the walkway, but remember that simplicity, elegance, and subtlety are never out of style.

Path Edgings

▣ Decorative Edgings

Think of a "decorative path edging," and perhaps the first thought that comes to mind is a line of large whitewashed stones set along the side of the path. Reject that thought.

How about stone benches set at regular intervals on one side and a border of flowering plants on the other, so those who wander down the path can sit down to enjoy the border?

Finely clipped low boxwood bushes are traditional path edgers and make an emphatic statement: Stay on the path.

Think about a fence edging the walk on which fruit trees are espaliered, offering an apple or a pear to passersby at harvest time. Or raspberries grown in a narrow band along the side of the walk, or a raised border filled with wild strawberries. Or think about edging the path on each side with hazel, which will grow to 15 feet (4.6 m) or more and whose tops can then be entwined to make a natural archway over the path.

If the path is made of gray or bluish stone, make a color contrast at the edges with something bright, like alternating the red stems of *Cornus stolonifera* with the yellow stems of *C. s.* 'Flaviramea'.

If the path is rough, coarse, light gravel, make a textural contrast by edging it with smooth, dark slate.

Create strips of humus-rich soil 2 feet (.6 m) wide along both sides of a moist, shady brick path, and set rounded river stones into the soil, leaving some space between the stones. Seed the soil with rich emerald-green moss that will fill in around the stones. In a sunny spot, set in larger stones and let *Thymus serpyllum*'s tiny creeping stems and leaves flow between, around, and over the stones and path edge itself.

Border a path with a line of *Pennisetum alopecuroides*—a foxtaillike grass that will invite passersby to brush their hands over the soft beige seedheads in the summer and fall.

Make a foot-wide, 16-inch-deep trench (30 x 40 cm) along both sides of the path and put 6 inches (15 cm) of sand in the bottom. Cut the bottoms from dark green winebottles and flame the cut edges of the bottles until they are smooth, then plunge the bottomless bottles neck-down into the sand—one bottle every 4 feet (1.2 m), with the open bottoms projecting a few inches above ground level. Now pour cement into the trench around the bottles until it reaches ground level. At night you can set lit candles into the bottles so the flame is slightly below the top of the bottle rim and protected from the breeze. They'll make an exceptionally nice green flickering glow to light one's way on special occasions.

Align a collection of beautiful pots along the edge of a well-traveled path and place flowering plants in plastic pots in them. You can easily change the color scheme by putting in new plastic-potted plants of various kinds as they come into flower.

Border a path with a narrow stream of recirculating water that slides down a slight incline. The structure can be made of concrete or mortared brick. Or build a narrow path edge of still water and stock it with goldfish and water lilies.

Alternate squares of grass and red and yellow tulips alongside your path, repeating them like this: grass, red tulips, grass, yellow tulips, grass, red tulips, and so on.

Edge a path with an 8-inch (20 cm)-wide strip of grass (or a grasslike plant such as dwarf liriope, ophiopogon, *Armeria maritima*, or *Dianthus* 'Tiny Rubies'). On the other side, away from the path, plant dark, humus-rich mulch with neat clumps

of hostas, bergenia, or other ornamental perennials.

If you run out of ideas, you can always whitewash a row of stones. But that's up to you.

◉ The Natural Look

If you've ever seen a well-used animal trail through a natural spot—such as a deer trail, or a place where cows walk in their evening queues, or a path through the woods where the local dogs run—then you know how a natural path should look. Plants and grass impinge on the trail, trying to reestablish themselves, while at the same time footfalls beat them back and pack the earth into a hardened surface.

Similarly, when constructing a natural-looking path edging, use some low plants and those that can take some foot traffic, interspersed with larger plants that

....

Left: *Marshall and Georgia McDaniels of Portland, Oregon, found a simple and inexpensive solution to the need for steps through their garden. The risers are timbers cut to size and held in place by 2-by-4s used as pegs. Gravel fills in behind each riser. The pathway is outlined with rows of pressure-treated logs cut to size and inserted vertically into the soil.*

Opposite: *If water-washed, flattened, rounded stones are what you have to work with, then go for it—as Timothy Maxson did at his home and garden in Bolinas, California. These steps are wide and generous, and set between high banks of fragrant lavender, helichrysum, erigeron, and chamaedrops. In winter, when these steps may need to be negotiated in driving rainstorms, the herbaceous plants will be cut back.*

will spill onto the pathway. If some of their leaves are stepped on, so much the better, for the natural edge is a place of battle between feet and foliage.

Make your edgings from the same kind of plantings used farther back from the path, rather than from a different set of plants used just for edging. If, for instance, you plant *Helictotrichon sempervirens*—a blue-green, grassy mound—so it makes a fountain that partially spills out into the path, then use some a few feet back from the path, so it looks like the walkway has

been made naturally by people trampling through the garden.

▣ Planting the Path Edge

One of the most beautiful and useful plants for the edge of a sunny path is mother-of-thyme *(Thymus serpyllum)*. It only grows an inch or so tall, but makes the most delightful spreading mat of inter-woven stems with tiny aromatic leaves and even tinier flowers that bees can't resist. It can take some foot traffic, too. Even better, like *Iberis sempervirens* and

Mazus reptans, it will grow and flower in the cracks between flagstones or pavers.

Another plant for between stone pavers is *Sagina subulata* (the light green kind is called Scotch moss, and the dark green kind Irish moss). It will take some foot traffic, and it's perfect for edging a path, spreading out from the edge between the stones until footfalls prevent it from spreading farther. Baby's tears *(Soleirolia soleirolii)* is similar, making a beautiful edging that will end where feet first land.

Left: *Simple steps made of slates and railroad ties are glorified because the designer allowed room for a variety of interesting plants to grow within the steps themselves. The stairway in this private garden in Southampton, New York, designed by Tish Rehill, delivers one to a walkway made of wooden slats, introducing variety into the design. The plants sound a lavender and purple theme stated by the lavender in the foreground and the tossing wands of butterfly bush (Buddleia davidii) in the background.*

Opposite: *The "stone" steps in Harland Hand's garden in El Cerrito, California, are actually made of cement by Mr. Hand—one of the finest garden artists in the world. Note how carefully he mixes dark areas of black aeoniums and red kalanchoes with gray-green blue oat grasses and succulent echeverias whose outer leaves carry echoes of the kalanchoes' colors. About half of the rocks in Hand's garden are artificial, yet are so effectively used it's hard to tell which are real and which are crafted.*

The large thin blades of *Miscanthus sinensis* 'Silver Feather' make a stunning, effective plant for a turn in the path, as its tall fountain of grass will hide what lies immediately beyond. Place it in the inner crook of the turn and lower, more colorful plants on the outer part. These might include *Potentilla* 'Gibson's Scarlet', *Campanula persicifolia* 'Telham Beauty', *Coreopsis grandiflora*, *Verbena* 'Homestead Purple', and other colorful workhorses of the perennial garden.

You could also go for the Dutch garden effect, edging the path on both sides with tulips, which you then plant up with colorful, all-season bedding annuals after the tulips die back. Cheery, colorful portulaca is an example of a good choice to follow tulips.

Shady paths offer great opportunities for pretty edgings. Lady's-mantle *(Alchemilla mollis)* is a standard edger, with wide, scalloped leaves and dull chartreuse flower billows. Plant Jacob's ladder *(Polemonium reptans)* under bleeding hearts *(Dicentra spectabilis)*. Virginia bluebells *(Mertensia virginica)* should go just everywhere, and slightly back from the path put columbines *(Aquilegia* hybrids). Clumps of red barrenwort *(Epimedium* x *rubrum)* will look good along the path edge, as will liriope. Intersperse everything with ferns—and if you don't know which fern to choose, choose the Japanese painted fern *(Athyrium japonicum* 'Pictum'), which is widely available from nurseries and catalogs, and airy maidenhair ferns. Behind these plants put tall blue clouds of meadow rue *(Thalictrum rochebrunianum)*.

◙ Lighting the Walkway

Garden paths that are an integral part of the approach to the house may need to be lit at night. As you plant up the edges of your walk, make sure to use low plants at regular intervals. Where the plants are low, put your lighting.

Choose lighting that throws pools of light onto the path, rather than back into the garden.

Contemporary lighting fixtures range from sci-fi (lights that look like flying saucers on stalks) to hand-beaten bells in the shape of flowering stalks with leaves. These metal flower shapes keep the garden theme in the day when they're not used, and do a fine job of lighting the pathway at night.

Outside lighting needs to be done to the specifications of your local building code, and is best installed by a certified electrician. It's possible to install a dimmer switch so you can adjust the lighting level to suit your needs or mood.

In areas of the country where the summer night-flying insect load is high, path lighting will soon be surrounded by clouds of moths. Thus drawn to your plantings, some will then lay eggs in your plantings that will hatch into leaf-eating caterpillars. Path lighting is thus best used sparingly in those areas—usually for a specific purpose such as when guests are arriving and leaving.

Steps, Stairs, and Ramps

Before considering different kinds of garden steps, we need to go over the rules about steps and stairways. This is human engineering, and the primary considerations are that the steps be safe, comfortable, easily negotiable, beautiful and decorative, and sturdy (see page 183).

There's a general rule about the relationship between risers (the distance of the step up) and tread (the distance from the lip of the step to the next riser). That is, the lower the riser, the wider and deeper the tread should be. The width of the tread (from side to side) can vary, but make it as wide as feasible, because narrow stairs look cramped and difficult. A

general rule is to make steps at least 4 to 6 feet wide (1.2–1.8 m) if two people are to walk abreast. Conversely, the higher the riser, the less deep and narrower the tread should be. This means that when you are climbing steep steps, make them narrow, high, and short in the tread.

Now for some numbers. Risers should never be less than 4 inches (10 cm), or people will miss them and stumble. Low risers should have deeper and wider treads—19 to 20 inches deep (48 to 51 cm) is standard for a 4-inch riser. On the other hand, risers should never be higher than 7 inches (18 cm). At 7 inches, the tread should be about 12 inches (31 cm) deep. Here's a general rule: twice the riser height plus the tread depth should equal 27 inches (68 cm). Thus a 6-inch (15 cm) riser would have a 15-inch (38 cm) tread, using this rule. And, in fact, these dimensions are standard.

Another rule: don't vary your riser or tread measurements in a flight of steps. This amounts to tricking people who may be looking at the garden. And if you have a long distance over which you're constructing steps, install some flat level areas where people can stop and rest.

When constructing steps, don't trust to numbers alone. As you rough out the stairs by excavating or filling on a slope, walk down it at a natural pace and make sure your natural step doesn't end up in midair, or right on the edge of a riser. Make sure that when negotiating the steps, your feet fall squarely and naturally on the treads. For a very long run of steps leading up a long slope, build in wide

terraces or landings here and there to give people a break as they climb.

Fit the type and look of steps to your garden. If you have a rustic garden in a shady woods, build a naturalistic set of steps using flat stones. The more formal the garden, the more formal the steps should be. Remember that steps don't have to whisk you from place to place: they can be part of a leisurely stroll through the garden. They may lead you up and down slopes and be constructed with wide flat platforms here and there as places to stop, where benches can be placed so people can sit down.

There's a problem with just cutting into a bank to make the first step, then building the next step, and the next, and so on until you're finished. The problem is that your riser-to-tread ratio will most likely be out of proportion, and your last step will most likely have to be jerryrigged or be of an odd height to reach the upper ground level. The way to avoid this problem is to measure your site first to figure out how many steps you're going to have to build, and then build them precisely.

Let's say you plan to put in steps on a bank that rises 6 feet over a 20-foot

Clipped cotoneaster and thymes decorate these magnificent steps in the Old Mill Dene garden at Blockley, Gloucestershire, England. Though the stones are of a type that can be pried up from the quarry in slabs, they are chipped and dressed for their role in the garden. The capstones and some of the rockwork are plastered in; other parts are dry wall construction. Using a variety of techniques to suit each step gives character to the finished whole.

The simplicity of this walkway and bridge is part of the Japanese theme in a Seattle garden. Two pieces of round pipe were set in the bottom of a form into which concrete was poured. As the concrete began to harden, the top was given the gentle curve that makes this structure so satisfying in its context.

240 inches (20 feet). You will have 10 steps with 15-inch deep treads, making 150 inches. That leaves 90 inches to be traversed, so one of the steps will be 90 inches (7½ feet) deep. Not only will all your proportions be right, but you will have made an interesting feature where you can place a bench, or perhaps a stone trough with succulents, or an urn with a mixed planting in it—the choice is yours.

A consideration when planning garden steps is to make sure your steps are visible. Use a light-colored material that contrasts with its surroundings so people notice the steps. Place urns or planters on either side to announce that steps are ahead. Have the tread overhang the riser by an inch or so to throw a shadow that sharpens the visibility of each step. Vary riser and tread materials so each step stands out clearly from the others.

distance, and you want to put in standard steps with 6-inch risers and 15-inch treads. You'll need 12 steps. But twelve 15-inch treads will only traverse 15 feet and you need to go 20. One possible answer is to deepen the treads to 20 inches so 12 of them make 20 feet. But 20-inch treads are out of proportion with 6-inch risers. Twenty-inch treads demand 4-inch risers. What to do?

First of all, a series of 12 steps has 12 risers but only 11 treads, as you don't count the top tread, which is where the path continues on its way. The answer is to go back to the plan of using 6-inch risers and 15-inch treads, except to make one of your 11 treads superdeep—actually making it a platform where people can stop and rest.

The distance to be covered is

◉ Steps of Natural Materials

Stone is the best natural material for steps, and there are various ways to use it. You can use flat stones as treads behind risers made of railroad ties or wood, and that arrangement makes a neat appearance. Or the entire set of steps can be made of stone. But lumpy, wobbly surfaces are out of the question. The prime consideration here is to create sturdy, immobile risers and treads. Footing must be absolutely firm if the steps are to be safe.

You'll need either very flat flagstones or dressed stones with even surfaces and flat edges. Dressed ashlars are expensive but make excellent risers. If they are higher than the size of the riser you want, excavate soil and put a bed of gravel or sand in the bottom, then set in your ashlar. Dig out the tread area behind the ashlar a few inches and put some sand in, then set in the flat stones so their surfaces are at the same level as the ashlar. Pitch the treads downward ¼ inch (.6 cm) from back to front so rainwater runs off and doesn't pond (and freeze).

If you're using railroad ties instead of ashlars, cut the ties to the desired width and drill 1¼-inch (3.2 cm) holes near each end. Set the ties in place and, using a hand sledge, pound 1-inch (2.5 cm) pipes cut 6 inches (15 cm) longer than the height of the ties down through the holes and into the ground, seating them just below the surface of the ties.

In narrow spots in rustic gardens, where people will be looking down at their footing, you can use overlapping natural flat stones, which can have some lumps in their surfaces. Even here, however, the stones should never wobble. One way to make sure they don't is to set flat stones into the soil on edge to form the risers, packing and tamping the soil down to within 4 or 5 inches of their tops, then

....

A finely crafted Japanese-style wooden bridge beckons one across a small stream in Jeanne Lipsett's garden in Norcross, Georgia. The sturdy flat stones on which the bridge rests are inter-planted with mondo grass (Ophiopogon japonicus) that further states the Japanese theme.

use concrete between and behind them to create a flat tread surface. This presents a decorative appearance, too.

◙ Metal and Glass Block

Using metal or glass block as steps is mostly a matter of whether you have them on hand. They are not the kind of materials you would go out and buy to make steps, but if you have a steel or iron staircase, it might fit just fine on a hillside and make a ready-made set of steps. Similarly, glass blocks, while usually used to make walls and partitions, are sturdy enough to be used as steps, unless someone drops a rock on them. They're chancy, but they could be a decorative addition to the garden.

◙ Mixed Materials

As with your path, mixed materials can be an exciting way to approach steps. Stone and cement, pebbles and glass, tiles and precast concrete—all these materials can fit together to enliven what might otherwise be a dull set of steps.

Try to develop a plan for mixing the materials, rather than mixing them haphazardly. You might use larger and larger flat stones with each successive step, or successively darker stones as you traverse the steps. Or you may intersperse tiles in cement, with each step's tiles

Light violet wisteria hangs from an arbor over a bridge at Monet's garden in Giverny, France. Its lightness and airiness is given a perfect counterpoint by the dark, almost red leaves of the purple smoke bush (Cotinus coggygria 'Royal Purple') that grows by the side of this slow-moving stream.

depicting a different kind of flower, bird, or abstract design.

◙ Ramps

A modest slope might best be traversed by a ramp. Although ramps look easy to negotiate, they tend to be more difficult than steps, since the surface is not level. However, if someone who frequents your garden is in a wheelchair, or if you want to provide access for the disabled, a ramp is an obvious solution.

Concrete or asphalt ramps should be constructed by a contractor, but you can build one of wood easily enough. Cut angles at the tops of 2-by-6 crosspieces whose bases sit level, so that 2-by-4s running the length of the ramp will lie flush against the angled cut. Or run four lengths of 2-by-6 lengthwise down the slope, and nail 2-by-4s crosswise across the ramp. This way you don't have to make the angled cuts on the crosspieces.

Bridges

Don't curse those low wet spots in your garden. They're going to give you an excuse to build a bridge or two so visitors can walk through the bog or water garden without getting their feet wet. And it's sure that if you build bridges, they themselves—even the simplest—will become major architectural features of the garden.

For bridges, siting is crucial. A bridge is best seen from over the water or from a path that approaches the bridge at a right angle. Bring your garden path to a spot

where the length of the bridge can be seen spanning the water in its entirety, and where the reflection of the bridge in the water doubles its image. Run the path around the water and up to the bridge, rather than bringing your path straight onto the bridge's walkway from the garden.

Bridges can be as elaborate as you care to make them. I've seen gardens with massive bridges made of brick and stone, and wonderful garden ornaments they are! They look as though the earth itself is shrugging and sending a ripple over the water. Formal bridges can be decorated with urns, lions, and mythical creatures.

These are bridges for the ages, however, and hardly the kind of bridges we will make through our gardens. For modest gardens, we need something that's also modest. The simplest is the Japanese zigzag bridge, built without railings, and made from posts and boards. Posts with cross braces support planks for walking. At appropriate places, a cross brace holds two sets of planks side by side. The second set then continues in a direction parallel to, and beside about a foot (.3 m) of, the first set.

◙ Arched Bridges

In the simple, rustic garden, choose a rustic design, such as a bridge made from unpeeled lengths of limbs used for railings on a bowed timber walkway.

The most important part of any bridge, even a simple one like this, is the piers on which the ends of the bridge sit.

These piers must be very sturdy and stable, made of stone and concrete, or concrete poured over reinforcing bars driven into the ground. Stone and concrete mortar piers look better than plain concrete if they are visible from the path, however.

If your bridge has railings, make sure all the railing posts are vertical. Nothing looks more awkward than posts fixed perpendicular to the curve of the bridge, which makes each set of posts jut out at crazy angles from the walkway.

Cutting and fashioning the supports for an arched bridge is work for the engineer and the master craftsperson. It is better to buy prefabricated arched bridge supports than to try to devise them. Many building-supply depots will have prefabricated bridge trusses, walkways, and supports—the basics on which you can work some personal magic.

◉ Flat Bridges

If the water to be crossed is shallow and not very extensive, there may be no need for railings. Just a flat support with boards nailed on may be all that's needed. Make sure the bridge is wide enough to avoid being treacherous, however. When there's no railing, the bridge should be low, just above the shallow water, and its width should be at least 5 feet (1.5 m) (see page 184).

◉ Using Color on Bridges to Accent a Garden

Certainly the natural color of wood will look good in any garden, especially after weather turns the wood to gray and silver. Nevertheless, a coat of light stain and outdoor varnish will help the wood retain a rich color that will harmonize with the garden's greens.

It's also possible to paint your bridge with harmonious colors, such as brown, green, and gray. White is very bright and tends to look very formal; you will have to plan carefully if the white is not to dominate a scene.

If you want your bridge to stand out, consider using a strong primary color instead of white. Red is choice and looks Chinese in a green garden. Yellow has a cartoony, Wizard of Oz look to it, while a muted shade of blue can be very quiet and beautiful, reflecting the color of the sky. Avoid purple or orange unless you have thought out the color scheme very carefully—although you could use a hint of these colors to accent large areas of more subtle color.

When using paint in the garden for any purpose, subtlety tends to be the best way to go, although a splash of bold color in the right place can be effective. You can paint the whole bridge, or just parts of it. A natural wood bridge with painted railing finials might be just the way to introduce a little bold color into an otherwise subtle scene.

◉ Decorative Railings for Paths, Walkways, and Bridges

One finds innumerable kinds of railings for use along difficult-to-negotiate paths, steps, and bridges, and they all afford the gardener a prime chance to add decorative touches to the garden.

Use wrought iron with stone or concrete, but not with wooden steps or pathways. When at all possible, use curving balustrades and railings, and save straight ones for formal steps and bridges.

Not every path or set of steps needs a railing, but if the going is at all steep or tough, add a railing that people can use to steady themselves. Functional railings are about 3 feet (1 m) high with a comfortable handgrip on top, no matter what kind of fanciful balustrade or ironwork is underneath.

Balustrades of highly pierced stone (which can be costly), waisted poured concrete in the shape of lathe-turned wood, wooden slats, and fancy posts relieve the expanses of greenery in a garden and show that the hand of the owner is working with nature to create the place of beauty.

When it comes to finding interesting and decorative railings, scour used building material yards, stop when you see a fine old house being dismantled, check your local building-material depots, and don't settle for the mundane.

Stepping Stones

◉ Using Natural Stone

In lieu of a bridge, consider stepping stones as a way of crossing a low, marshy spot or a slow stream. Don't try to get people across a swiftly moving stream on stepping stones—that's inviting a misstep that may leave your guests sitting in the rushing water, spluttering. In a marshy spot or very slow stream, how-

Lacy dogwood flowers and foliage are complemented by the meanders of the decorative railing that gently leads down a hill at Barnsley Gardens in Adairsville, Georgia. Both functional and beautiful, the railing borders a wide, inviting path of wood chips.

ever, a wet foot is about the worst mishap that awaits.

One of the best features of using flat-topped stones for steps across a wet place is that, if placed well, they can look as if nature placed them there herself. Yet when you negotiate your way across them, they seem to have been perfectly placed (which, of course, they were).

The secret to a naturalistic look is to avoid placing stepping stones in a straight line. They should be placed here and there, roughly in the direction across the wet spot, but varying from a straight line from this side to that. Also, they should be placed in groups of two or three, with certain stones placed alone. There should be gaps between groups of stones or singles, but never farther apart than someone negotiating them can easily reach (see page 184).

▣ Truncated Pillars

They're not easy to find, but they do exist—pillars that have been sawn into rounds. These make fabulous stepping stones and are extremely decorative, as their fluting makes a nice vertical contrast to the water, which always tends toward horizontal. Check building-supply depots, marble yards, and businesses that sell stone. Sometimes demolition contractors will have, or know where to get, stone, concrete, or marble pillars. Stonecutting facilities can saw them into rounds for you. You'll probably want to hire a small band of muscular young men to move these rounds into place, as they will be extremely heavy.

◎ Sawn Rock

Stone quarries and similar facilities often saw rock for special purposes, and you can inquire as to what they have on hand, or whether they can saw large rocks into flat-bottomed (and flat-topped) stepping stones for you. The flat bottoms are convenient for making a sturdy footing in water or mud, and the sawn flat tops are

....

Right: *A stone path steps right through a small water feature in the Lind family garden in Portland, Oregon. The bright stones are wisely contrasted with dark soil, making the stones very easy to see and helping to insure good footing. Light gray cobbles edge the waterway to emphasize its presence, so that the entire design illuminates what's going on, helping visitors to easily negotiate the path.*

Opposite: *Some solutions in the garden are so simple, elegant, practical, and right that it's a wonder they aren't more widely used. A perfect example is found in this Portland, Oregon, garden, where the outflow from a slow-moving stream isn't carried under a bridge, but drains out between closely spaced stones in a composite walkway.*

very ornamental. Again, however, choose stone that is gritty enough so that it won't turn slick when wet.

◎ Rounds of Tree Trunks and Log Sections

For temporary stepping stones, you can use rounds cut from a large log. Their flat surfaces will anchor nicely on the wet bog or stream bottom, and the submerged portions will last for years. The parts that are exposed to air will rot out first, but using rounds buys you time until you can install more permanent stepping stones or a bridge.

A log sawn in half lengthwise and laid, flat side down, in the bog or stream makes the kind of bridge we all traversed as children. It might be fun to cross your stream in the same way now, except be prepared for wet feet, especially as the bark begins to rot off and slip away underfoot. You can have the log sawn lengthwise by taking off slabs top and bottom, giving a flat surface to walk on—but that's cheating. It's the threat of a wet foot or a tumble into the stream that makes the log bridge exciting. I remember crossing a log bridge—really just a tree that had fallen across a swift stream—one January day many years ago. It was bitterly cold, and you could see the water swirling and puddling as it rushed underneath the skin of ice that reached most of the way across the stream. My foot slipped and I fell up to my chest in the stinging cold water. A mile and a half from the nearest house, I immediately started running, figuring that if I stopped, I'd freeze to death. By the time I got to the house, my clothes were frozen stiff as cardboard—but I was fine. The running kept me warm. Your log bridge needn't provide such an adventure, but it will be exciting to step gingerly across it.

◎ Other Innovative Ideas

Round sections of drainage pipe set on end into the wet area or stream can be filled with soil and planted with tough grass. These will recall the hummocks of grass that grow in bogs, while giving the visitor a grassy footing across the area. And the grass roots will be able to reach down to the constantly wet soil at the bottom for their water, so watering won't be necessary. You can also fill pipe sections with concrete.

You can construct a pathway to traverse the area, but don't let it become a barrier to easy water flow. There's positive drainage and water movement, even in what appears to be the standing water of a bog, and blocking it with a bermed pathway will cause a severe environmental disruption. Instead, first put down one or more round sections of drainage pipe, then build the bermed pathway over them, so water can flow freely from one side of the pathway to the other.

A bermed pathway offers the gardener opportunity. Its sides and the edges of the top can be planted with a variety of plants or set with tile or stone to make the berm decorative as well as functional.

For a fun way of getting across a rather narrow little stream or wet spot, look up to see if there's a tree limb overhead. If there is, fix a rope to it that dangles just above the wet surface, and which people can reach from the edge of the wet area. With a bit of a running start, they can hold onto the rope and swing over the wet area with ease. This may not be possible for the infirm, but most folks of ordinary physical abilities can negotiate it.

If your garden's wet spot is a small pond, build a raft or have a small boat at the edge so people can row or pole across. This is fun, but you know that the raft or boat will always be on the side that you aren't. Is the answer two boats? Perhaps it's no boats at all, just a path that travels the rim of the pond. I like the path solution, as you can take people on a wonderful little journey through the reeds where the red-winged blackbirds whistle and the frogs jump ahead of you.

CHAPTER FIVE

Garden Furniture

The temperature is delightfully warm and the air is filled with the garden's perfume. Shafts of midafternoon sunlight slant through the trees, spilling golden coins on the ground. You are so wonderfully tired after finishing the refurbishing of an annual garden, and there, slung between trees, is your wide, inviting, colorful, restful hammock. You sit on the edge, push off with one foot to get the hammock rocking, then swing your feet up into the woven mesh, leaning back and stretching out to your full length. You close your eyes and feel warm and coddled, as though Mother Nature were holding you in her arms, and a bit of sunlight flickers on your closed eyelids, making red flashes. That's all you remember until you awake, refreshed, to the song of a bird.

If the garden is a place of relaxation and refreshment, then our garden furniture allows us to sit, or lie down, or take a cup of tea amid the spring lilacs.

The problem is, where to put this furniture?

Think first about the comfort of the people who will be using it. That means that there should be shade, whether provided by a canopy of trees overhead or by an umbrella that's part of the table-and-chair set.

Furniture works best in its own discrete area. Provide a patio or base of crushed gravel or tile; give it a setting that puts it into perspective. Make the size of the patio or ground under the furniture proportional to the pieces in the group. Picture, if you will, a table with umbrella and four chairs set out in a lawn. The fur-

niture looks lost, like a raft of furnishing afloat on a sea of grass, adrift.

Instead, tuck the furniture into a nook where it can relate to the structure of the garden: between trees, or in a garden room, or by a fence overgrown with clematis or honeysuckle.

Sometimes an individual piece of furniture is called for, to be used as a place for visitors to sit. To decide where to place such furniture, walk your paths and consider where you'd like to stop, either because you need a rest, or because there's a view that's worth an extra look, or because there's a particularly beautiful garden setting that needs study, or because the spot is uniquely comfortable.

Think also about using garden furniture as a focal point. Large pieces like wooden benches draw the eye and can be placed at the ends of pathways or down an allée of trees or potted plants at the focal point of the garden composition. Using a piece of man-made furniture as a foil to all nature's greenery that way is an especially good idea, because simply more shrubbery or flower beds might not make the focal point strong enough. The contrast of bright wood with green leaves and flower colors is a strong one—just what you need at a focal point.

Decorate your garden with furniture that you think matches the style of your plantings. Eschew the aluminum chaise longue. Keep an eye out for the well-made and artistically crafted. Cheap outdoor furniture will only degrade the beauty of its surroundings and possibly give visitors reason to question your taste. Better to have only one beautiful and expensive bench in a garden than a lot of unlovely and inexpensive furniture.

Right: *Keep your eyes open for any garden furniture as special as this scallop-back bench in Chris Wotruba's garden in La Mesa, California. It's been given a gray antiqued surface, as has the bird feeder with sculpted quail in front of it. Its design is classy yet informal and comfortable.*

Page 100: *When pathways invite us to walk them, a comfortable garden seat should then beckon as a place to relax. This cushiony seat in Jane Paulson's garden in Santa Barbara, California, places the visitor beneath a fiery explosion of bougainvillea.*

Benches and Banquette Seating

Wood for Outdoor Use

Wood for outdoor furniture needs some very special qualities: it must look good after it weathers; it shouldn't crack or splinter; it should be impervious to rain; and it should be proof against rot and mildew without having to be impregnated with dangerous chemicals.

Some of the most popular woods with these qualities are redwood, cedar, and tropical hardwoods such as teak and mahogany. Of these, redwood is the least desirable. Although it is weather-resistant and slow to rot, it does have the bad habit of splintering, and redwood splinters always seem to promote little infections in the skin. Some manufacturers carve and give their redwood a paint or cement patina, actually rubbing wet cement into the porous surface of the redwood, which helps seal it and toughen it. But bare redwood can be splintery, and all redwood is soft wood that doesn't take a knock without denting. Finally, redwood has a very limited range, from Big Sur on the California coast to southern Oregon, and not far inland, and it has been logged to just a remnant of its former expanse. While it's still being logged, many people would like to see the logging pressure reduced so the trees can regenerate over more of their original range.

Cedar is usually harder than redwood and less prone to splintering, and it raises fewer environmental concerns. Classic English garden benches are

often made of cedar, and it's altogether a worthy material.

Tropical woods such as teak and mahogany present something of a problem to the gardener, for the spirit isn't quiet that must wonder whether the bench in the garden has been crafted from virgin rain-forest timber. I think most gardeners, with their innate respect for nature, would not have delicate and important ecosystems destroyed just so

they might sit upon a teak bench.

More and more of this wood is being raised on timber plantations, however, especially in Southeast Asia. If you are going to buy garden furniture made of tropical woods, make sure that the wood comes from plantation-raised trees. Many reputable manufacturers give that information proudly in their marketing materials.

Garden benches are usually 4 feet to 6 feet (1.2–1.8 m) long. The best have curved, slatted seats. The slats allow rainwater to trickle through, and the curve fits the human bottom more comfortably than a flat surface. Probably the most famous

Too elaborate a bench in this setting at Bourton House Garden, Bourton-on-the-Hill, Gloucestershire, England, might detract from the beautifully espaliered firethorn (Pyracantha 'Mojave'). The simple deacon's bench will do—and in a neutral color, too. The dark burgundy leaves of Cotinus coggygria 'Royal Purple' and the pink pelargonium in the pot at lower left subtly accent the rest of the scene.

While some garden benches are placed inconspicuously in the landscape, others are a focal point. This flower-petaled wooden bench at Rancho Los Alamitos in Long Beach, California, is definitely the latter, as the courses of succulents and flat cobbles form rays that pull the eye right back to the bench's echo of a setting sun.

garden bench is the Lutyens bench, named for the British architect and designer Sir Edwin Lutyens. Lutyens learned "simplicity of intention and directness of purpose" from the renowned garden designer Gertrude Jekyll, who took these cues from John Ruskin. Lutyens designed buildings, grand cathedrals, and even the city of New Delhi in India, but today his bench—at once formal, pleasing, and inviting, with a high back that combines arabesque-like curves and horizontal slats in satisfying proportions—has carried his name around the world.

Other popular styles of benches have vertical slatted backs that radiate up and slightly out from behind the seat. There are gently curved hardwood and pine benches, large enough for two or three people, that fit into a curved corner or along a gently curved pathway. Elaborate benches include those with handles on one end and a large wooden wheel on the other, so the whole bench can be moved, like a wheelbarrow, from spot to spot. Some rustic benches are made from pine poles about 6 inches (15 cm) in diameter.

The simplest bench is perhaps that made by pouring cement around two long uprights in back and two shorter ones in front, fixing them together with cross-pieces connecting each back upright to the front ones. A single board across the crosspieces serves as a seat, and a single

A wooden bench seat in the form of a boomerang graces a small seating area at a garden at Elk Rock, Lake Oswego, Oregon. A visitor who sits on this seat gets to gaze at a gorgeous red-leaved Acer palmatum *whose beauty is doubled by its reflection in the water.*

board across the uprights serves as a back-rest. This design is as simple as can be, and yet if the bench is made carefully from good wood, it will be handsome and serviceable in any garden.

Benches may be turned into ban-quettes by the addition of pillows for more comfort. The best kind for outdoor use are plastic all-weather cushions available at hardware and home-furnishing stores. Rain simply runs through their expanded plastic mesh.

Metal seating

Metal seating—usually wrought-iron or cast-iron benches for permanent out-door use, or steel for patio, lawn, or pool furniture—can be used to suggest a certain era in the garden.

Cast-iron seating, usually enamel-painted to prevent rusting, suggests the Victorian era, especially when the designs are in the Gothic mode. Victorian tree seating—cast-iron benches that wrap around the trunk of a tree—is still found,

Left: *Victorian-style cast-iron furniture, with its arabesques, makes a charming place to take high tea in the Wesley Rouse garden in Southbury, Connecticut. Very sturdy-looking stone steps lead up to the patio, behind which a well-pruned apple tree twists and turns.*

Opposite: *A Lutyens-style bench with matching chairs and table has silvered with exposure to the elements and makes an inviting place to sit in this formal garden in Birmingham, Alabama. A pair of morning glory towers flank the bench.*

usually painted white, but when you are browsing for a tree seat, lift the sections to make sure they are of heavy cast iron, and not light aluminum replicas that are too flimsy to stand up to use. White paint will draw the eye strongly in a green garden, especially on a large piece such as a tree seat, so choose your spots carefully and make sure that the furniture is an adjunct to the landscape, rather than a visually dominant element.

Cast iron isn't as strong as wrought iron or steel and requires more metal, making it clunkier and heavier than other metals. Wrought iron can be drawn out into more airy and interesting shapes than cast iron. Look for wrought-iron pieces with graceful curves and arabesques. I've seen love seats and benches in wrought iron that suggest Paris in the 1920s, others that give a mid-20th-century look. Avoid tubular aluminum benches, which are flimsy and have a cheap appearance.

I like metal benches with iron mesh for the back and seat. Rainwater runs right through, and there's plenty of air circula-

tion through the mesh to keep you cool on hot, sticky days. White-painted iron mesh will stay cooler than black mesh if the piece is sited in the sun.

▣ Stone and Concrete

Once, in a hillside garden under many high birch trees, I found a stone that made a perfect bench seat. Although it was natural, it looked as though it had been carved like a wooden seat, with hollows on either side of a slight central ridge. I searched and found two stones to support the seat, and simply laid it on top of the supports. It was wonderfully comfortable, and every time I visited that part of the garden, I'd sit down and watch the sunbeams dance on the fluttery birch leaves. Because it was so simple and so comfortable, it became a treat to use, as though somehow I'd beaten the system. Of all the seats I've ever sat on in a garden, that simple stone seat is my all-time favorite.

I tell this story to encourage you to keep your eyes open for flat stones that might make simple stone benches in the garden. Such benches are unobtrusive, made of natural materials, fun to find and sit on, last forever, and cost nothing but a little of your time.

One of the advantages of creating benches from native stones is that you can pack soil between the stones and plant succulents, iberis, Roman chamomile, or other rockery plants to bring a bit of the garden into the bench, even as the bench brings a bit of civilization into the garden.

More elaborate carved-stone or cast-concrete benches also last just about forever. Concrete, especially, is often found cast with garden-related decorations in

Opposite: A plain stone and concrete bench has a timeless, elegant appearance. At the garden of Mrs. R. Paice at Bourton House in Gloucestershire, England, such a bench is glorified by being situated in a setback of ivy beneath a mountainous ornamental pear, flanked by the rounded mounds of evergreens, and facing a formal arrangement of clipped boxwood hedges.

Right: Carefully selected and assembled pieces of driftwood make an odd but comfortable garden seat in Judy Wigand's garden in San Marcos, California. How wonderful that someone saw the decorative and practical possibilities of driftwood and found a way to bring the idea to reality.

relief, such as leaf and vine figures, grapes and other fruit, or floral designs. Some of the finest cast endpieces (which support wooden seats) are fashioned into female busts, swans, or mythological personae like griffins and satyrs. When you find a piece you particularly like, snap it up, because the good ones tend to go fast, and most of this kind of garden furniture is cast by folks who are either far away and unable to make a steady supply or are making odd dollars between jobs.

Of all the materials for garden furniture, I prefer stone and cast concrete. I like their substantial look, and the fact that these natural native materials (concrete is simply ground-and-cooked limestone mixed with gravel, after all) are usually of a color that blends well in the garden—visible, but not gaudy or bright. Stone and concrete wear well, but they do have one drawback: they stay wet longer after a rain than many other materials.

Mixed Materials

Most garden centers and large hardware or home-furnishing stores sell mixed-material garden bench kits. These are typically fashioned from two iron endpieces enameled black and antiqued with verdigris paint, with a prefabricated back of wood and iron latticework or similar design, and seating made from long lengths of durable hardwood that bolt to the iron endpieces. I've put one of these together in less than an hour of easy work, except for the one bolt that didn't quite

reach the hole provided for it in the endpiece. After some deliberation (wondering whether I would break the wooden seat slat or the metal endpiece), I used a trusty hammer to drive the bolt home without incident. The finished bench is quite graceful and sits on a brick patio that flanks a shade garden of astilbes, ferns, Solomon's seal, and daphnes.

It's also easy to find cast-concrete endpieces with boards for the back and seats, of the type commonly seen in public parks. These have a familiar appeal but aren't particularly graceful. You could use one as a park bench nostalgia feature by placing it along a paved path and erecting an old-fashioned lamppost next to it, then putting in some shrubs. The old lampposts had a wonderful way of throwing a pool of soft light down around them, and the bench might be the perfect place to kindle the flames of passion with your sweetheart.

Finally, let me encourage your creativity in mixing materials by making benches of your own design. Wrought iron, cast iron, stone, concrete, wood, and steel can be found in scrapyards, and a bit of poking around might give you a fine idea for a way to build an odd bench that decorates your garden with ingenuity.

Tables, Chairs, and Other Seating Furniture

Garden and Patio Tables, Chairs, and Swings

The standard patio table is round, with an enameled steel frame and a glass top through the center of which is a hole to receive an umbrella. It's not a bad design at all, but just the beginning of what's available for use on the patio or in the garden.

Since the tables and chairs serve several purposes, one of which is to decorate your garden, choose only those with beautiful, sculptural, or classic lines—furniture that you think shows an easy grace in its design, or that you think will be the perfect architectural accompaniment for a specific garden site. Here's another chance to use your aesthetic sense.

Chairs often need outdoor cushions. Choose these carefully, too, for they can easily clash with the patio's setting or the garden. Flowered prints in soft greens and mauves and lavenders tend to work with anything the garden may be doing at the time. You'll find that bright colors, all the way to white, become harder to work into a subdued scheme, and the brighter the color, the harder it is to justify in the garden setting.

I have a fondness for old-fashioned folding chairs, of the kind Kenneth Branagh so anachronistically and ridiculously struggled with in his film adaptation of Shakespeare's *Much Ado about*

Nothing. Despite their reputation as the outdoor furniture equivalent of a Chinese puzzle, I find them not only easy to set up and fold down, but comfortable as well. The only real problem with them is that when they are made with fabric, the fabric tends to rot out after long exposure to the elements. Which means that woven nylon seating material is the way to go.

Adirondack chairs create a Gatsby-esque look, while sprung tubular steel chairs—the kind with the metal seats that spring up and down because they are

attached to a single steel tube that's bent in a modified S-shape—have a 1950s look to them.

Today, garden furniture is a booming field for innovative design. Some designers work in quantity, like Ralph Lauren, who turns out reliable and pretty wicker patio tables. Other artists emphasize limited editions. Audrey Hemenway, for example, has a unique table with a freeform planter in the center to fill with herbs, so guests can add spice to their lunches. Some of the more lavishly designed substantial pieces are from McGuire, which has showrooms in major cities (and upscale enclaves) in America, while very trim and clean furniture is being made by Brown Jordan in El Monte,

Above: *Although somber, the dusky purple of the cushion on this outdoor chair at Joy Wolff's garden in Healdsburg, California, is the perfect accent for the flowering lavender behind it and for the roses on either side of the fence's doorway: 'Phyllis Bide' on the left and 'Felicia' on the right.*

Opposite: *Baskets of pelargoniums add color to—and creeping ivy sneaks up on—the beautifully designed, hand-finished, and hand-carved patio furniture that embellishes the brick patio at Jody Honnen's garden in Rancho Santa Fe, California.*

California. Reed Bros. in Sebastopol, California, makes hand-carved outdoor furniture in a variety of designs. Other notable designers are Giati, Munder-Skiles, and Palacek. By all means, investigate what modern furniture makers are doing. It's very exciting.

New designers have introduced new materials. One of my favorite pieces of ultramodern outdoor furniture is Brown Jordan's garden chaise of wrapped steel tubes and woven seating and backing made of Resinweave, a space-age material that won't peel, crack, or fade, and that comes in wonderful colors, such as a rich dark green that allows the chaise to be placed anywhere in or near the garden.

Designers of patio and garden chairs are going way beyond the traditional and creating functional pieces that haven't been seen before. Sun-or-Shade makes the "Chaise de Soleil," which resembles a huge chair with cushions, with a baby-buggy-type retractable canopy. A leg rest flips up in front if desired, the top has infinite positions controlled by push buttons, and the whole thing revolves 360 degrees on swivels so that you can relax, read, snooze, or daydream in full protection from the wind and sun. This rather ungainly contraption is immensely utilitarian and comfortable.

A fine addition to the garden is an old-fashioned Victorian swing—basically a bench suspended from a cross-piece set upon two triangular uprights. Set among roses and mock orange, the trestle swing makes an excellent decorative element.

Above: *A simple design incorporates a raised platform, comfortable chairs, table, and an awning to keep off the sun in one unit at Jane Paulson's garden in Santa Barbara, California. A moment's respite there offers long views of the surrounding scenery, and a pot of pelargoniums on the left and bougainvillea on the right provide color.*

Opposite: *The comfortable chairs and stylish umbrella at Joy Wolff's garden in Healdsburg, California, provide a welcoming, shaded place to enjoy the 'Phyllis Bide' rose that smothers the railing and post behind them.*

Less suited to the garden are bulky children's play sets and large swings for the kids. These really need an open space away from the garden, where the children can romp and play without damaging plants.

No matter what your furnishing needs, remember one simple rule: garden and patio furniture should be of materials and colors that enhance the scene, rather than clash with it.

Umbrellas, Jalousies, Awnings, and Overhangs

Just when the garden reaches its peak of growth and bloom in June, the sun begins its intense summer sojourn, often making garden visitors uncomfortable. Yet you don't always want to be tucked back under the canopy of trees for shade. Thus the garden umbrella, either as part of a table or as freestanding element, brings shade where it's needed. The best kind—although not the most expensive —surmount poles with hinges that allow the umbrella to be tilted and moved in a circle, following the sun's movements. This kind often has a valuable feature: a crank that quickly allows you to collapse the umbrella if the wind kicks up.

Among the more expensive umbrellas are large sun umbrellas with bamboo or tropical-wood frames, canvas coverings in natural shades, and solid poles. These usually don't have cranks and have only two positions, open or closed. They look appealing, but the kind with hinges and cranks are far more practical in my opinion.

There are freestanding canvas pavilions that can bring shade to the occasional luncheon on the lawn. If the garden spot is just outside the house, surrounding a patio, jalousies and awnings attached to the house can afford some shade on the patio. A space under an overhanging cantilevered building or deck may also be a refuge on hot summer days, and a place to install a shade garden.

Outdoor Cabinetry, Bars, and Barbeques

◉ Freestanding Service Areas

There's something deliciously hedonistic about a nicely crafted area for having cocktails or dinner al fresco. How much more delicious when this area is integrated into the garden.

Service bars and barbeques are often built near swimming pools, but they can also be built out into the garden. I once saw a yard where a tiled pathway led back into a circular grove of trees. Among the trees were flowering shrubs like rose of Sharon, viburnums, and roses. In the center was a grassy area, and at the middle of that was a raised tile-and-brick barbeque. Benches around the barbeque pit allowed it to double as a place for a campfire on warm nights. It became one of the most visited spots in the garden.

Closer to the house, a patio can be edged with an outdoor service area that forms a buffer between the patio and the garden. This is a good place for potted plants that help ease the transition from patio to garden, and bring some greenery onto the patio. Protection from the weather for grills, refrigerators, dry sinks, and so forth must be provided. Look into waterproof coverings that can be pulled over the service bar, or built-in cabinet doors that can be closed.

....

Opposite: *The drainage hole near the base of this fine old urn shows that it once served a practical as well as decorative function. The embossed device on its surface is the Medici coat of arms. Now it sits in a sprawling* Fatsia japonica *in James Morton's garden in Savannah, Georgia.*

Below: *The variegated hosta and prickly-leaved* Cyrtomium falcatum *make a pleasant setting for the star of this garden passage: the jar with a fine, funky glaze. This arrangement is at Porter Carswell's garden in Savannah, Georgia.*

▣ Service Area with Pass-through to House

A large open window or counter from the kitchen outside to an enclosed conservatory or covered patio, all flanked by greenery and gardens, is a lovely idea. Continue the flooring inside the house out through french doors to the patio, and continue the patio construction right out into the garden—an arrangement that brings the inside of the house outdoors, and invites the garden into the living areas.

In times gone by, the conservatory was a glassed-in place, sometimes heated in the coldest months, where tender plants were kept. Modifications of this idea are still a good idea. New materials aren't as breakable as glass, but allow all the beneficial wavelengths of light through to encourage good plant growth. Although artificial grass is usually cheesy at best, here's one place where it just might work. A friend of mine built a conservatory—today we might call it an attached sunroom—on the southwest side of her house. Large doors on the wide wall facing the garden can open so the room doesn't overheat on hot days, and the glass panels in the ceiling can be cranked open for air movement, too.

In the early spring and late fall, when the world is brown, her sunroom flourishes, stocked with potted plants of all kinds (I remember one particularly sweet pot of *Hoya bella* hanging out its clusters of waxy white five-pointed stars with red centers). She would set a table for lunch there, and the artificial grass carpeting gave the illusion of a lunch outside on a summer day. It wasn't elaborate, but it was very effective.

Vases, Jars, and Pots

Every gardener should have a collection of favorite containers for decorative use by themselves and for planting. They can be vases, urns, jars, pots, troughs, and anything that looks beautiful and will hold soil and give good drainage.

Let's look first at their uses.

Probably more than any other item, plants surrounding pretty containers or in them decorate the garden. If a passage looking down a walkway seems bland, a group of three or more large pots with brightly colored annuals like

115

pelargoniums, big plumpy begonias, impatiens, or the like will soon fix that.

If a spot needs a splash of red for a time, move in a pot full of verbena. If it needs yellow, in come the marigolds. When your sun-lovers reach full bloom, move them into a shady spot for a time to prolong their bloom and to bring sunny-colored cheer to a lugubrious spot. When the bloom subsides, move the plants out again, or have some pots in the sun in reserve for exchange.

Grow plants and bulbs in plastic pots, and then move them close to the house when they bloom, slipping them into your favorite permanent containers, such as fine terra-cotta or cast concrete urns. When the flowers begin to fade, back out to the holding area they go, where they can be heeled under mulch with their leaves exposed to gather sunlight and manufacture food for next year's bloom, without disrupting the scenery near the house.

Potted plants can be used to edge a path or create an allée; in baskets, they can be hung down a line of trees. I know a path where the gardener hung baskets of fuchsias every 10 feet under a living canopy of slender laburnums that bent at the top to meet, touch, and intertwine their topmost branches.

Terraces and patios come to life when decorated with lots of fine pots in various colors and glazes. The same can be said for a broad sweep of steps. Just make sure that you don't have single little pots sitting by themselves in isolated spots, looking lonely and out of place.

Left: *Pots and jars don't have to contain anything to decorate a garden. Here at Jack Lenor Larsen's garden on Long Island, five magnificent jars give a bold and dominant look to an otherwise plain patio.*

Below: *Three excellent pots, all similar—although not boringly identical—in shape, hold colorful petunias and chrysanthemums in a close trio at Sonja Gauron's garden at Le Perray en Yvelines, France. The importance of this group of pots is emphasized by the sunburst setting of gravel and firebrick of which they are the centerpiece. Over time, their earthenware surfaces will acquire beautiful patinas.*

Opposite: *Three simple and decorative elements create a masterful bit of design in Ryan Gainey's garden in Decatur, Georgia. Bricks interplanted with grass are arrayed in a starburst pattern around a circle of violet and white violas in full bloom. The ceramic flowers that decorate the pot in the center pick up where the violas leave off. A well-thought-out but oh-so-simple idea.*

Buy large pots and group them by threes and fives.

Shy away from orange clay pots. Many other colors such as dull ochers and beiges can be found. Glazed pots are lovely. Just make sure all of yours have positive drainage.

The classic style and shape of the Medici urn is priceless when it's original, but look around garden furniture stores for the polyethylene kind. These copies of 19th-century originals come in black, green, and white, and they are almost indistinguishable from the metal originals.

Strawberry jars are ubiquitous and seldom given the right treatment. Plant them with something tall and upright in the top space—I use phormium 'Maori Sunrise'—and plants that will spill and trail from the side pockets. Strawberries with their trailing runners are excellent, but mine now has violas looking very pretty. Or put in culinary herbs that you can pinch when making dinner. Pot marjoram, thymes, summer savory, and oregano will produce heavily in a strawberry jar. Dittany of Crete would look exceptional spilling

Above: *A magnificent window box graces a private residence in Charleston, South Carolina. The plantings include the light blue—almost white—flowers of plumbago with yellow lantana and pink pelargoniums, interplanted with variegated ivy.*

Opposite: *In areas too cold for echeverias, sempervivums, also known as hens and chicks, are fine substitutes. Planting several types, as here in this concrete trough in a private garden in Vancouver, British Columbia, gives variety to the assemblage. Sempervivums look particularly good among and between rocks.*

out of the top of a jar planted with other herbs in the side pockets.

You'll need to have very good soil in the pots—freshly made compost is a wonderful amendment that gives actively decaying organic matter to the potting soil and keeps it loose and spongy. You have to water potted plants often—even every day in hot weather. Feed potted plants every few weeks with diluted fish emulsion as a soil drench and seaweed extract applied to the leaves.

Some of the prettiest flower arrangements are living; that is, they are a group of plants planted together in a large pot. Trailing helichrysum and upright phormium interspersed with a plant that produces profusions of flowers, like diascias, make wonderful companions in a pot on the back porch. A pot-grown vine will climb from the garden to reach your porch, throwing color and scent to everyone who walks by.

Really good pots only look more beautiful as they acquire time's patinas. Mosses, lichens, discolorations from water, even a little grime from the air—all these add character to a pot. Terra-cotta is especially good at acquiring a patina, although most of what you get at the early stages is white salt crusts (easily reduced with a quick brushing with a steel or stiff-bristled brush). Italian terra-cotta pots are expensive, but nothing looks as good. They come in ornate or simple designs. They're all so beautiful, and decorate the garden or patio so well, I never know which to choose. If the terra-cotta is above your budget, look for the fiberglass planters made to look like terra-cotta. Unless you inspect them closely, they're hard to tell from the fired ware, and their designs are often very similar. The classic terra-cotta designs can also be found in gray to whitish cast-cement or concrete planters.

The deep color of glazed pots is always welcome in a garden, giving a sophisticated and artful effect. Look for earth tones of soft greens, browns, ochers, reds, and yellows.

Keep your eyes open for great plant containers other than pots designed for the purpose. You may find a fired porcelain chimney pot, or a galvanized, figured metal box, or anything else you think has enough merit and utility to warrant a new life as a featured container.

 ## Windowboxes and Planters

Windowboxes are wonderful! Not only do they dress up a window when you're looking at it from the outside, but they presage the garden views beyond when you're in the house looking out.

My personal rule is that you can't overplant a windowbox. Stuff it full of upright and trailing plants. Use fragrant ones like stock, trailing ones like *Helichrysum petiolare*—both the silver and lime-colored

Use windowboxes on sunny walls, especially those facing well-used paths and walkways. Remember that windowboxes are simply planters attached to windowsills. Detached and set on stoops, along the edges of patios, and on the edges of rooftops, they also serve an ornamental purpose.

Besides windowboxes and pots, there are many other types of planters. Some planters are meant to attach to walls or fences, like sconces, while others look best partially sunk into the ground. Woven-wire baskets lined with plastic mesh can stand free on wire legs; there are also wire plant-holding benches and a whole range of hanging baskets for decorating porches or hanging from tree limbs in the garden. I once saw a garden pathway that looked sumptuous because the gardener had filled hanging baskets with brightly colored begonias and then hung them from limbs above the path. It was a very decorative and effective idea.

One of the best-looking planting containers is the English stone trough. Originally designed to hold water for livestock, these troughs today are made especially as garden containers. They come with drainage holes drilled in the bottom,

versions—and ivies, especially Kenilworth ivy. Annuals such as *Thunbergia alata* (the black-eyed Susan vine) will add an interesting color to the box. Make it profuse and awash in color and fragrance. Plants like *Coreopsis verticillata* 'Moonbeam' will stay neat, resist drought, and bloom all summer. Don't forget the primroses.

Like any container, a windowbox will dry out quickly, so keep it well watered. Use metal brackets to hold it an inch or so away from the wall, especially if the wall is made of wood. Good soil and frequent drenchings with fish emulsion are required, because many plants crowded

into a small space, all competing, will need extra nutrients.

Because water will filter through and out of the bottom of the windowbox, it's a good idea to plant the ground under the windowbox with something that will hide the drippage. A bed of annuals is fine, but their color may detract from the windowbox. A bed of herbs, such as thyme or sage, might be better if the spot is sunny, or *Pachysandra procumbens* (if you're tired of *Pachysandra terminalis*), if the spot is shaded by the box above. Like most planters, windowboxes themselves will need a sunny spot to look their most floriferous.

and are filled with soil and gravel. They are usually about 3 feet (1 m) long and 1½ feet (.5 m) wide (or thereabouts) and planted into miniature gardens with rocks, alpines, and, most frequently, succulents.

Wheelbarrows, Wagons, and Tools

Old abandoned carts, wagons, wheelbarrows, and even garden tools give a sense of age and history to a garden. An old wagon can be used as a staging area for many potted plants, and the wheelbarrow may be filled with soil and planted up with annuals and trailing flowers or vines. Bush morning glories, succulents, verbenas, and perennials like *Saponaria ocymoides* can be planted in a wheelbarrow, as long as the soil is kept moist and the plants are put in the ground to overwinter (plants exposed to deep frost in pots and elevated places like wheelbarrows are much more prone to die overwinter).

Be careful with these decorations, however. Use them sparingly, because too many look cutesy-pie, tacky, or worse.

Left: *An extremely vigorous specimen of* Campanula poscharskyana *has decided to take its rest in an old chair made of bent saplings in Geoff Beasley's Sherwood, Oregon, garden designed by Michael Schultz. The chair looks as though its age might preclude further use as a seat for people, but for the campanula, with its cheery blue stars, it functions just fine.*

Opposite: *An old wheelbarrow serves as a planter for asters and foxgloves in Carol Dickinson's garden in San Diego.*

121

CHAPTER SIX

Gazebos, Pergolas, Arbors, and Trellises

To the terms *gazebo, arbor,* and *pergola* we could add *kiosk, pavilion,* and *summer house*—all the buildings one can add to a garden to make a place of cozy refuge from the elements and a place for relaxing and dining. These are different from utilitarian buildings like potting sheds and greenhouses, which can also be charming in the garden setting.

There's some dispute about the nomenclature of garden buildings. I will give you my interpretation. I see no real difference between a gazebo and a pavilion. Both are open structures set in the garden as a place to be sheltered from the rain or the sun. Though they are usually round or many-sided, they can be rectangular or even three-sided.

Kiosks are also related to gazebos and pavilions, although I think of them as usually small and highly ornamented in a way that suggests oriental decorative techniques. They might be used to serve food and drink for guests to enjoy in the garden.

An arbor, on the other hand, is an arch of some sort—either freestanding, or as part of a fence over a doorway, or as an overhead structure attached to the house or other building. In any case, an arbor's primary function is as a scaffolding on which climbing plants can grow.

Take an arbor and repeat it down a walkway, and you've got a pergola. The ruins of a magnificent pergola exist at San Simeon, William Randolph Hearst's fantasy estate near Cambria, California. This series of arbors is almost a mile long, with the arbors connected by beams the whole way, over which fruit trees and fruiting vines of all kinds were trained, and down whose pathway Hearst and his guests could ride their horses, stopping to pluck ripe fruit from the abundant foliage overhead. It must have been quite a place in its heyday.

Summer houses are more substantial, to my way of thinking. They may have actual walls, doors, and windows, and may be appointed inside with a daybed or couch for napping. In essence, a summer house is a room built out in the garden for privacy, and for a person to enjoy the sweet scents of the garden day or night in the comfort of a sheltered room.

All these garden buildings add architectural elements to nature's greenery, making fine contrasts. Even the most modest will, however, draw the eye strongly away from the plantings, so it's important to think carefully about your building site.

Above: *'American Pillar' roses grown on a multi-arched arbor above a well-made dry wall of dressed stone make a classic border for a paved walkway at Longwood Gardens in Kennett Square, Pennsylvania. This would be an effective way to dress up a driveway, too.*

Right: *This flower tunnel, or floral pergola, has its archways far enough apart that sunlight will always fall to the path beneath. Honeysuckle (*Lonicera japonica *'Halliana') climbs the archways while mounds of pink saxifrage and blue nepeta edge the walkway. A close look at this walkway at the garden of Mr. and Mrs. George Lane Fox at Bramham Park, Wetherby, West Yorkshire, England, reveals it to be a stunning example of rustic stonework and a perfect foil for the border.*

Page 122: *A nicely designed gazebo with a copper roof and paint that helps it merge into the evergreens around it makes a great place to view the magnificent valley and snow-capped mountains beyond the property of Sam Bibler in Kalispell, Montana.*

One of the most important considerations is that the building be in scale with the other buildings and the gardens and grounds around it. A tiny potting shed in a grand garden won't do, nor will a big and bulky pavilion crammed into a small backyard. Good proportion, as in any work of visual art, is essential.

Give the garden building a dark backdrop. A stand of Irish yews would be an impressively dark background for a garden building. But any dark green plants with dull leaves set at least partially in the shade will do the trick. When the eye is drawn to the garden building, it doesn't do to have its lines broken and rendered hard to read by a dappled background.

Associate a garden building with other landscape elements so that it doesn't look like it's been dropped onto the lawn or into the garden haphazardly, sitting

forlornly with no reference to what's going on around it.

Start by looking at the lay of the land, and deciding where a vertical building would look most suitable. Perhaps it would be best tucked just under the lee of a bank or hill. Or perhaps it stands proudly atop a small rise. Are there large trees nearby with which it can make a dance? Site it where it feels most satisfying in terms of formal artistic composition, and where it also makes the most sense.

A good rule is to site any garden building along the margins of the garden. That way, it will help to define the garden's boundaries as well as leave the center of the garden open for plantings or lawn.

When you create a garden building, don't scrimp. And don't buy flimsy arbors or archways held together by staples from a staplegun. Such pieces of gimcrackery are a waste of money and will lean and then crash down as soon as you get a good growth of vines on top. You're not building a child's playhouse for just one season's use, but a substantial piece of garden art. Give particular attention to the roof, which should have some stand-out feature, like a dome, or filigree work that creates a fine silhouette against the failing light in the evening sky, or simply cantilevered beams that hold hanging baskets of fuchsias. Build as large a structure as you can, keeping it in proportion to its surroundings—this advice suggests generosity, a quality that goes well in the garden. Use the very best materials you can find. They'll pay off in looks and longevity. Overbuild, or the plants that grow and twine and twist up the poles and beams will rot them and tear them apart in short order.

Suit the structure to the kind of garden. A Japanese summer house looks best in a Japanese garden, a quaint English pavilion in an English garden. An American garden might have something sturdy and simple, of rustic materials. One of the nicest garden structures I've seen is at an acquaintance's house in California. He constructed a summer house with a real English thatched roof, importing both the reeds for the thatch and the thatcher himself from England to do the job. The result is spectacular—and was, of course, costly.

Make sure that the outbuilding, arbor, or pergola in some way is coordinated with the architecture of the house. Match the main house in materials and in the look of the building—especially if the

Left: *The white running fence, teahouse, simple stonework, water, and sparse plantings of evergreens all strongly sound the Japanese theme in the Lind family's private garden in Portland, Oregon. For all its simplicity of form and style, it still becomes a very decorative place.*

Opposite: *This stunning arbor at Carol Dickinson's garden in San Diego is a delightful structure at back of the house. A beautiful brick wall that's a backdrop for a planting of foxglove rises to a gloriously white arbor arrayed in a semicircle and planted with red roses and other vines. Notice the hanging lanterns under the crosspieces and the interesting way in which the topmost joists are finished at their tips.*

structure is attached. If it doesn't match, it will appear like a bit of prettiness grafted on as a decorative afterthought, rather than an integral part of the garden.

Finally, and most importantly, realize that, like the garden itself, a garden building is art. It needs to look as though it's always been there and always will be there, because you can't imagine the spot without it. Just as one can't change a word in a poem without changing everything in the poem, the garden building must give one that sense of particular-ity—that the building is perfectly suited to the space, and has a practical as well as a decorative value there. It should not look like something turned out cookie-cutter style, but like something built for that space: inevitable, inspired, and inviting to use.

◉ Gazebos, Pavilions, and Summer Houses

If you are to have a gazebo or pavilion, be generous. Make it large enough to seat a garden party. Give it individuality, even if you do purchase it prefabricated from a catalog. Consider hiring a carpenter to make one aspect of it unique.

Give your gazebo a spot at the edge of the garden rather than out in the middle of the lawn, where people having tea would look like the figurines on a wedding cake. Place the structure where a path will lead naturally up to it so that it becomes a sheltered place in the garden, rather than something out in the lawn that one must climb up out of the garden to reach.

I suppose I'm describing a summer house rather than a frilly gazebo. I want my gazebo (or pavilion or summer house, as you will) to have some strength to underpin its romance.

My dream summer house will have large windows that can be thrown open to allow all the balmy air to enter, but be closed on cold, windy, rainy days when I want to hunker down and read my Emerson. In case you haven't read *your* Emerson in a while, let me suggest that you get a copy of his essays and go to your summer house on a fragrant spring afternoon; then slowly, with relish, read his essay entitled "Circles."

Here we have a garden decoration worthy of the name. If a garden is a collaboration between nature's green plants with their genetically programmed agendas and a gardener full of human desires, then the summer house or gazebo is the place to which the human repairs when the backbreaking work is through, dirty hands and sweaty brow are washed clean, the garden has been overseen and enjoyed, and now it's time for some human pleasure—tea and cakes, kisses and hugs, or daydreams.

◉ Arbors and Pergolas

The simplest arbors and pergolas are made of steel rods bent into a variety of shapes. Here I'd include the wirework rose bowers, which are essentially half gazebos/half arbors on which climbing roses can grow and smother the open frame. You can find these steel structures as round arches—or a series of round

arches forming a pergola that can cover a featured walkway for as much distance as you like. You can also find them as steel *tuteurs*, a French term meaning protector. These garden ornaments look like an open umbrella on which a climbing plant can twine up and then spill over, throwing protective shade below. The Monet arch has straight vertical sides and a slightly rounded top, while the top of a gothic arch forms a point, like hands in an attitude of prayer.

When the arbor or pergola is made of wood, take a tip from the way Italian garden architects do it and make it sturdy—as sturdy as the timbers that frame a house. Set the uprights into holes that are then filled with cement. Set the crosspieces on end along the top so they have substance from a distance. Vines such as wisteria and especially trumpet vines will literally tear flimsy arbors and pergolas to pieces.

If the arbor is to create an arch over a fence, consider wooden supports with curves sawn out of them to make a moon

gate effect under the arch. Make sure the arbor is architecturally related to the fence, however. Build seats under the arbor, or grow two vines from opposite sides so they intertwine over the central part of the elevated arch. Right now my cup-and-saucer vine and *Clematis montana* are blooming and holding hands on the arbor over the gate to the swimming pool in a charming effect.

An arbor over a patio can be attached to the house, and allows one to grow favorite flowering vines over the top that provide shade as well as beauty. Or mix

grapes with a favorite flowering vine so that fruit and flowers are held just above the heads of those using the patio.

Any featured walkway, especially one that ties the house and deck or patios to the garden, is a fine place for a pergola. Its upright supporting pillars or posts give you the chance to plant many vines, a different one at each post, for a circus effect (honeysuckle, clematis, roses, morning glories, moonflowers, wisteria, schizophragma, crossvine, Carolina jessamine, jasmines, passionflower, grapevines—the list goes on). But for the classical look, repeat the same flowering vine at each post, all the way down one side, and train fruiting trees or vines up and over the top from the other side. Wisteria is the most beautiful of all the vines, in my opinion, and fragrant as well. It only blooms for a couple of weeks, but what a couple of weeks they are! Choosing a rose that flowers and continues to flower all season—like 'Cécile Brunner' or 'Climbing Iceberg' or 'Don Juan'—at least keeps you in flowers for the summer. Mixing roses and wisteria is an excellent idea, because the wisteria is over before the roses really get going. Just don't let the wisteria overwhelm the roses and choke them off.

Opposite: Perfectly balanced and harmonized design characterizes this gazebo, pond, and trellised fence in Arnold Steiner's garden in Birmingham, Alabama. Masses of white flowers along the brickwork by the gazebo are provided by oakleaf hydrangeas (Hydrangea quercifolia).

Above: Water lilies (Nymphaea) and mounds of little white erigeron bloom sweetly beside a Victorian-style gazebo at the McDuffie family's private garden in Monticeto, California. The gardener has color-coordinated the gazebo, the fence, and the plantings to produce an oasis of quiet and dignity.

▣ Trellises

My personal rule for trellises is that you can't have enough of them. These multipurpose structures support all kinds of climbing plants. They make a barrier so that kids, animals, and stray adults don't wade through your shrubbery.

They shade the sun from outdoor garden rooms, and even, when covered with ivy, create living walls. They allow you to decorate the wall of a building, and help enclose an arbor to make it into a functional pavilion. Used atop fences, trellises extend your privacy upward but allow you to see over the top of the fence.

A vine twining along a trellis-topped fence adds a softening touch.

On a still more utilitarian note, trellises give your vegetable garden a place for peas, sweet potatoes, cucumbers, and melons to get up off the damp, mildewed ground. They also work well to block the view of an ugly shed or screen off the view into a neighbor's yard.

Trellising comes in prefabricated latticework panels that are easy to erect or attach to upright poles. Trellises also come as painted or unpainted rectangles or vase-shaped sprays of wood. Steel and iron trellising, often painted with black enamel, is available.

A diagonally patterned lattice trellis gives a more decorative look, and vines like to climb up its diagonals, helping to accentuate them. A trellis made entirely of vertical slats gives a formal loft to the sides of an arbor. Purely horizontal trellising is rare; it accentuates the length of whatever it is attached to or sited by. Square or rectangular grid patterns give a solid, architectural look and might be appropriate on a sheltered pavilion tucked away down a shrub-bordered pathway, or on the sides of a potting shed.

Then there's the elaborate trick-of-the-eye trellising that's designed to look

Left: *The prettiest little stone path leads up to an arbor drowning under a magnificent* Solanum jasminoides—*commonly called the potato vine because its flowers resemble those of the potato. A statue beyond is placed so it's framed by the arbor as you come up the cobbled steps. This is Corine Gruenwald's garden in Rancho Santa Fe, California.*

Opposite: *At Deepwood Gardens in Salem, Oregon, lime green boxwood clipped to a low hedge leads the visitor to this arbored garden gateway, glorified with a crown of* Clematis montana *var.* rubens *in full, exquisite bloom. A young hawthorn* (Crataegus) *flanks the gateway. The choice of deep forest green paint on the fence and gateway helps to pull the scene together.*

like an arched pergola that recedes away from you, but in reality is constructed flat against a wall, giving only the illusion of depth. Such structures were not uncommon in the Victorian era, and are still found—there's a beautiful example at the M. H. de Young Memorial Museum in Golden Gate Park in San Francisco.

The French art of treillage involves complex latticework arranged in the form of pavilions or pergolas or even elaborate small houses. In a very full garden with a floriferous look, treillage might be just the decorative touch that's needed—but it is the opposite of simple, deriving its charm from its complexity.

A trellis placed against a wall can be backed with a mirror, which adds a feeling of depth and movement behind the latticework as one walks by. This doesn't always work to perfection, but you can give it a try if you have a mirror that will serve.

Use trellises freely in the garden because they give you that most cherished of attributes: a vertical dimension. Most architectural verticality in the garden is stationary—fences and walls that can't be moved without a lot of work and deconstruction. But trellising is easy. You can place it where you want it for now and move it where you want it later without much trouble at all.

I find that with trellising that has support poles on its sides, the easiest way to erect it is to drive a length of metal pipe into the ground and either insert the poles into the pipe so they're held steady, or leave about 18 inches (46 cm) of pipe above the ground and attach the poles to the pipe with clamps or wire. If the exposed metal and wire looks too obvious, get out that can of forest green enamel and dash some on. You'll hardly notice it when it's painted.

Left: *An arbor attached to a house is a great way to decorate an otherwise dull side yard or back of the house. Here, at Joy Wolff's garden in Healdsburg, California, the attached arbor is draped with 'Blush Noisette' roses, 'Hagley Hybrid' clematis, a wisteria, and in the background another clematis climbing the post on the left. Window boxes decorate the house, and borders of herbs and perennial flowers flank the path.*

Opposite: *A large example of French-style treillage (trellising) makes a stand-alone statement at Sundial Herb Garden in Connecticut. The look is very symmetrical and formal, and cleverly uses vertical space greater than square footage in the garden. It's planted with* Rosa gallica, *a French rose of ancient heritage.*

CHAPTER SEVEN

Statuary and Garden Art

Garden art may be grouped into three broad categories—formal, semiformal, and informal.

Formal art is classical statuary and serious sculpture, such as a fine marble statue of Diana and her hounds. Its themes are usually classical and its feeling serene. Its impression is one of timeless beauty.

Semiformal art is mainly decorative, not overly serious, but nicely executed. A good example might be a bronze statue of a boy fishing at the edge of a lily pond. Its themes are usually taken from daily life. Its feeling is often nostalgic. Its impression is sweet or delightful.

Informal art is fun rather than serious. Plastic dinosaurs hiding underneath the hosta leaves are an example. Informal art is usually campy or humorous, creating an amusing or cute impression.

This chapter focuses on formal art and some semiformal art. The emphasis will be on using it in the garden, rather than suggesting individual pieces.

After all, beauty is in the eye of the beholder, and you are the judge of what is most beautiful to you. If a piece of art appeals to you, by all means acquire it if you can.

Most statuary and fine art makes a strong impression in the garden. If the material contrasts with the surrounding vegetation (such as bright cast concrete or marble), the impression is heightened. So when you consider siting a piece of sculpture, think about placing it at a focal point. This may be down the length of an allée or walkway, where a path curves, where the shrubs and trees lead the eye, at the end of a

length of fence whose perspective narrows as it recedes.

If a statue is out in the open, on the lawn for instance, it runs the risk of seeming isolated and unrelated to the garden. It's also never out of view, and that can become tiresome. Fine art also renders the lawn useless for such activities as playing catch or whiffleball. You don't want to drift back to catch a ball and run into a marble statue.

Perhaps the best strategy for siting garden statuary is to place it where it must be discovered. Shield it from constant view by placing it back behind shrubs, so that someone finds it when walking the garden path. Think of your garden as discrete rooms, and place no more than one piece of garden art in each room. Remember that not every

Above: *A small stone lad in 19th-century garb carries his basket of fruit among lamb's ears* (Stachys byzantina), *small-leaved cotoneaster, and* Viburnum tinus *at Jeff Drum's garden in Charlotte, North Carolina. Sited among shrubs and perennials, stone statues soon become swathed in greenery, often with charming results.*

Left: *This lovely figure—Flora, the goddess of flowers, or Pomona, the goddess of fruit, or simply the sculptor's model—gazes serenely at the ferns and hostas at her feet. She's held gently in the arms of an eastern hemlock (Tsuga cana-densis) in Ginger Epstein's garden in Atlanta.*

Page 134: *A marvelous sculpture,* Lioness and Cub, *by Hope Yandell, is installed at Brookgreen Gardens in Murrells Inlet, South Carolina. The set-ting beneath the spreading, sagging limbs of the live oak tree couldn't be more perfect, as humps and dips in the limbs repeat the humped backs of the lioness and her baby. The tension of responsi-bility as well as leadership in the musculature of the lioness is palpable, while the cub's muscles are flexed in play. Placing sculpture in the garden requires great care and careful scrutiny of the site to achieve this level of quality.*

garden room needs a piece of man-made art. Some spots should feature the plantings themselves as art.

I like to walk through a garden for the first time and be surprised by delights the gardener has hidden for me there. That is certainly true of garden art. Once I know a garden, I can then choose to visit the artwork or pass it by. Art that's too exposed is forced upon the visitor.

Although statues can be placed in a bower or be surrounded by plantings, I don't think it's a good idea to allow

them to be covered even partially by plants such as climbing roses or vines. I feel there's something unkempt and decadent about a carved figure being overgrown by plants. Most art was made to be seen in its entirety, and an overgrowth of plants prevents that.

Classical statuary is best discovered in a glade or grove, a garden room, or bower. Although such statues often refer to a rich mythology or history, that context is long gone, and the literary content has mostly vanished with time. Some of

your visitors may know why Narcissus is peering into the pool of water, some may not. So it's best to treat formal or classical statuary in a formal context, giving it its own space, placing it where it will be in

A small putto oversees the bathing birds in this charming bit of cast statuary in the Ireland garden in Birmingham, Alabama. The surrounding azaleas are pretty, but they grow about as close to the figure as should be allowed. Unless the azaleas are pruned, poor putto may disappear among the blossoms next year.

proportion to the plantings around it, and where it can be seen and enjoyed so that its formal artistic qualities of line, weight, balance, and technique are enhanced.

Any piece of garden art should be in proportion to its garden setting. A foot-high (31 cm) statue would be lost in the grass of a large yard. An eight-foot-high (2.5 m) reproduction of Zeus would be ludicrous, if not scary, in a small garden room. Satisfying and elegant proportion is at bottom a matter of taste. Think of the garden setting as a frame within which the garden art is the focal point of the picture. Stand at the spot where the art will most often be viewed and visualize it in place. Make sure it is entirely within the frame in such a way that there is plenty of room around it, and that it is placed somewhat off center.

Representations of classical figures don't have to be in the style of ancient sculpture. They can also be contemporary. I've seen a marvelous depiction of

....

Right: *The elemental Native American woman with her bowl was created by R. C. Gorman and is entitled* Wawona. *She sits on a deck that encircles the oak trees at the Van den Berghe garden in Danville, California. If a garden has architectural features such as this elevated deck, sculpture may be more at home there than out among the greenery.*

Opposite: *A stylized brass piper plays his tunes among the branches of a perfect plum tree in Walter and Fran Bull's garden in Columbia, South Carolina. The color of the plums and the yellow buttonlike flowers of* Santolina chamae-cyparissus *by his feet reflect the rich metallic cast of the statue.*

Flora, the Roman goddess of flowers, sitting atop a white pillar in an overgrown garden in Berkeley, California. This Flora was sculpted from redwood just a few years ago, and her body is elongated like a Modigliani nude. It is also splitting apart from the head downward, with a green shoot emerging from the chasm as though the goddess were the personification of a seed. The artist intended the work to be didactic, teaching us how to grow as a plant grows.

I recently saw another piece of contemporary sculpture that makes a cultural as well as horticultural statement. It consists of three ceramic skeletons—*esqueletos*—set amid succulents like echeverias, cacti, and brightly colored plants such as *Zauschneria californica*, red verbena, zinnias, and marigolds. The tableau makes a reference to the Mexican Day of the Dead. The skeletons are cast and fired white enamel, and they look perfectly happy and at home among the plants of the western deserts and Mexican tropics.

It's my feeling that cultural references work best when they are located in or near the areas of their cultural influence. While our Mexican *muertas* are suitable in a California landscape, they would be out of place in Nashua, New Hampshire, or Cherbourg, or West Essex. In areas where the cultural roots run back to northern Europe, I find that classical subjects still look best.

When placing a matched pair of sculptures, use them to flank a featured plant or area of hardscaping like a set

of steps. This is the "bookends" strategy. Another strategy is to hide one from another, such as around a bend, where one is encountered and then the second is discovered soon after. This is the "echo" effect.

In a time when the classical myths still gave strong structure to thought, Batty Langley, in his *New Principles of Gardening* (1728), wrote:

There is nothing adds so much to the beauty and grandeur of gardens as fine statues; and nothing more disagreeable than when wrongly plac'd; as Neptune on a terrace walk . . . or Pan, the god of sheep, in a canal or a

fountain. But to prevent such absurdities, take the following directions:

For open lawns and large centers, Mars, god of battle, with the goddess Fame; Jupiter, god of thunder, with Venus, goddess of love and beauty; and the graces Aglaio, Thalia, and Euphrosyne; Apollo, god of wisdom, with the seven liberal sciences; the three destinies . . . Demergorgon and Tellus, gods of the earth . . . Pytho, goddess of eloquence; Vesta, goddess of chastity; Voluptia, goddess of pleasure; Atlas and Hercules, god of labor.

For woods and groves: Ceres and Flora; Sylvanus, god, and Feronia, goddess of the woods; Actaeon, a hunter whom Diana turn'd into a hart, and was devoured by his own dogs; Echo, a virgin rejected of her lover, pined away in the woods for sorrow, where her voice still remains; Philomela, a young maid ravish'd by Tereus . . . afterwards transformed into a nightingale . . . and lastly, Nuppaeae, fairies of the woods.

There must have been a great deal of wrong placement in centuries gone by. Alexander Pope in his *Fourth Epistle* (1731) mocks Lord Timon for the placement of statues in his garden:

The suffering eye inverted nature sees,
Trees cut to statues, statues thick as trees;
With here a fountain, never to be played;
And there a summer-house, that knows
*   no shade;*

Here Amphitrite sails through myrtle
  bowers;
There gladiators fight or die in flowers;
Unwatered see the drooping seahorse
  mourn,
And swallows roost in Nilus' dusty urn.

Not all classical statuary is based on the gods and goddesses of ancient Greece and Rome. At Powis Castle in Wales, 18th-century cast-lead figures of pipers and peasants in rustic dress are every bit as classic as any nymph or satyr. However, Powis Castle has its share of classical statues, such as Hercules battling the Hydra, which is a copy of an original statue created in the 17th century for Versailles. Statues of animals, both mythological and real, are popular as garden art. Boars, stags, elk, lions, wolves, bears, and foxes lend a wild note to the garden. I recently purchased a stone fox that sits wide-eyed and ready to run under a large pieris, and his natural grace and poise are a welcome sight every time I pass by.

Formal garden art usually needs a pedestal to emphasize its classical line. A statue of a Nike standing firmly with laurel wreaths ready for victors' heads would look ludicrous standing on the ground, but becomes imposing on a pedestal.

Pedestals themselves can be art—adorned with carvings in bas relief of figures or laurels, or drapery and fruit. A pedestal doesn't necessarily need a figure atop it to be good garden art. Europe abounds with pedestals topped with carved finials—pure decoration.

A well-known example, carved about 1720 by Andries Carpentiere, is at Wimpole Hall in Cambridgeshire, England. This is a pedestal with an extremely elaborate finial decorated with leaves and floral designs, plus heads of goddesses looking out all around the top.

Semiformal pieces often have a narrative as well as artistic component that speaks directly to the contemporary viewer. A bronze of a young girl taking a step might be placed on stepping stones by a stream, or placed in some situation where the step adds to the story that the statue tells. A bronze of a young boy running and about to launch a gliding airplane into the air needs to be placed where the boy would actually have room to run, not back in a small glade with tight boundaries.

Semiformal art often doesn't require a pedestal, but tells its story and plays its part directly on stones or on the earth. Some semiformal pieces are meant to be set into the ground, such as the tongue-in-cheek "lawn croc"—three pieces meant to be set into the grass, giving the appearance of a crocodile surfacing and disappearing along its length as if swimming under the grass.

Abstract and modern art pieces are usually unrelated to the plantings around them, and need, if not an actual pedestal, an area of gravel or base of stone to give them a context. As an exception to the rule of keeping art out of the lawn, some modern pieces are really best seen when placed on grass. You might want to reserve a special piece of lawn to display these.

Above: *The sculpture is the marvelous* Boxing Hares *by Sophie Ryder, placed in the Hannah Peschar Sculpture Garden, an installation created by landscape designer Anthony Paul in Ockley, Surrey, England. The energy expressed in the statues even takes the eye away from the display afforded by the rhododendron in the background.*

Opposite: *This striking installation is a sculptural piece of art called* Heightened Perception. *The unnatural red color yanks the eye down the aisle of grass flanked by azaleas. Jack Lenor Larsen designed this essay on perspective for his garden on Long Island. The optically active red serves as a visual magnet among all the quiet greens.*

Original art is expensive, especially so if the pieces are old. Few of us could afford the actual 19th-century Nikes mentioned above, four of which recently sold at auction for close to 30,000 dollars (£18,000). But thankfully for us art lovers and gardeners, historical reproductions are a booming market these days, and many firms are making beautiful copies of classical pieces from the great gardens of Europe.

England, with its centuries-old traditions, is the source for many licensed reproductions of classic garden pieces from grand estates. Architectural Heritage is a Gloucestershire company with distribution in the United States through Garden Accents. Among their treasures is a statue of Pan seated on a tree stump, playing his pipes. They also offer two stone lions to flank a garden bench, copied from the 15th-century lions in the Piazza San Marco in Venice.

Also in England, Haddonstone makes fine reproductions of grand pieces, which are offered in the United States through Euro Antiques of Bethesda, Maryland, among other outlets. Besides reproductions of famous English pieces, this company offers a copy of a 15th-century Venetian trough, and a horse head found at Civitavecchia, Italy, and passed down through the Medici family.

Another firm of note is Chilstone, represented in the United States by New England Garden Ornaments. It offers a wide variety of statuary and pedestals,

Sculpture Placement Ltd. of Washington, D.C., handles Seward Johnson's bronze sculptures. Johnson spent nearly a lifetime painting before turning to his whimsical depictions of everyday people doing everyday things. These semiformal pieces are life-size, lifelike statues of common folk, many at their gardening chores. They are bronze, but fitted with actual clothing that's coated with resin for protection from the weather. Johnson has four garden-related statues—a young girl with a watering can, a man in a fedora pruning a tree, a woman with kerchief and trowel on her hands and knees, and a gardener in overalls transplanting a seedling from a pot into the

plus urns and other garden decorations. It reproduces a greyhound made for Lord Townshend at Raynham Hall, and a sphinx from Syon Park, plus recumbent right- and left-hand lions cast from 18th-century originals.

An American firm that specializes in historical garden sculpture from the grand country homes of Europe is Design Toscano in Arlington Heights, Illinois. It has a collection of angels, gargoyles, and classical statues.

Winterthur Reproductions in Delaware and the Ryan Gainey Collection in Atlanta, Georgia, also produce reproductions of classic garden art. Winterthur's pieces are usually made of resin plastic (resembling marble) to stand up to the weather.

Above: *A ponderous piece of granite is pierced and its circumference polished, then it's set on a slab of stone in Jack Lenor Larsen's garden. The sculpture is entitled* Moonscape Bench. *Despite the weight of the stone, it seems to surf on its stone slab, ready to lift off from the lawn like a moon rising into the sky from behind the mountains of the earth.*

Left: *Like a chess piece that has come to life and stepped into the garden, this ceramic chimney pot adds the human touch to Maggie Svenson's garden in Charlotte, North Carolina. The branches of* Cryptomeria japonica *descend from above to meet the grassy leaves of* Liriope muscari *rising from below. A spot of color is given by a patch of violas.*

ground. It would be startling to round a corner in a garden and discover one of these folks at their work.

Garden art isn't just statuary, however. Wonderful originals and reproductions are available for plaques, bas-reliefs, globes, and a hundred other art pieces that reflect the artist's appreciation of nature and classic forms.

My advice is not to settle for any piece of garden art—statuary or otherwise—that isn't absolutely first rate. That doesn't mean it necessarily has to be expensive. Found objects of satisfying design may be discovered in garage sales, flea markets, and even junkyards. Here's a chance to use your sense of aesthetics and sense of play. Just make sure that the garden art is in proportion to its surroundings, is in balance with the garden's movements, and is not obtrusive by virtue of shape or color. Finally, remember that a little garden art relieves a lot of plants. Just enough is always better than too much.

....

Sundials, which catch sunbeams and turn them into information, have accented gardens around the world for millennia. Many have garden themes engraved on their surfaces. Here in Barbara Chevalier's garden in Bolinas, California, two rocks mark a sundial whose pointer slants away. Flowery Campanula portenschlagiana, *accented with tiny white daisies of* Erigeron karvinskianus, *flows around these elements.*

Creations for Other Garden Inhabitants

We tend to think of gardens as places where human beings interact with plants, but nature doesn't stop there. She populates the garden with birds, mice, voles, shrews, possums, snakes, skunks, bats, raccoons, chipmunks, rabbits, squirrels, dogs, cats, and deer; with toads and frogs; with earthworms and cutworms and saw worms; with beetles of all kinds; with ants and grass-hoppers and crickets and fireflies; with caterpillars and ladybugs and spiders; and of course with bees and flies and wasps, hornets, bumblebees, hoverflies, moths, and butterflies.

All this is to the good. In fact, the more kinds of creatures in the garden, the stronger the web of life, the tighter the fabric of interwoven strategies for sur-vival, and the healthier the garden.

When we garden, we disturb the natural order of things. When we dig, we turn over a soil profile that may have been decades or centuries in the making, disrupting all the denizens of that shovel-ful of earth. The vegetation on that spot won't grow back as before, and the first plants to reestablish themselves are the opportunistic weeds such as briars and broad-leaved ragweeds.

If we use pesticides to kill insects, the fabric of life is torn. The insects don't re-turn in the same proportions, and the first to come back are the plant-eating pests.

Yet in a properly maintained garden, where disruption is kept to a minimum, birds and beneficial insects will gobble up pests. Snakes will eat mice. Birds will eat weed seeds. Skunks will eat cutworm grubs. Nature will fill her niches with her

creations, life will be diverse and plenti-ful, and health will be the result.

The gardener's job is to make sure that the garden is a hospitable place for the diversity of creatures who can live there. That means pure water and shel-ter, seed-bearing plants, some local weeds. It means putting away the pesti-cides, herbicides, and fungicides that are so disruptive and cause such slaugh-ter in the garden. It means building health in the garden from the ground up by using composts and manures and green cover crops and mulches that decay into rich soil.

Then, no matter what the creature, it will find a home in the garden. If it begins to build up its populations toward pest levels, its natural enemies will keep it in check.

◎ Birdhouses, Birdbaths, and Bird Feeders

Birds are always most welcome in the garden, helping to reduce insect populations, flittering with quick motion in the quiet bushes, filling the air with song, splashing their colors here and there. The ideal situation for the greatest number and variety of birds is the mixed habitat of the woodland border, which is often found in good gardens. In the background are the high-canopied woods with deep shade within. Bordering that are large evergreen and deciduous shrubs, and in front of them, mixtures of annual and perennial flowering plants and small shrubs. These in turn edge the lawn. In such places, birds find food and shelter.

Right now a nesting pair of olive-sided flycatchers has returned to our garden for the second straight year. Last year they built their mud-and-twig nest under our high front deck, out of the reach of

Right: *A simple birdhouse nailed to a fence post among fragrant roses must be a paradise for a lucky bird who will find thrips and rose chafers to peck at right outside its door. The rose will benefit in other ways, too, as the detritus from the nest and from bird comings and goings will enrich the soil below. This scene is in Charles Cresson's garden in Swarthmore, Pennsylvania.*

Page 144: *Birdhouses have several important functions in the garden. They are decorative, but they are also nurseries for birds that snap up insects, lace the garden with their silvery songs, and add color and movement to the trees and shrubs. This double-decker invites birds to Jody Honnen's garden in Rancho Santa Fe, California.*

the other garden creatures, and raised a brood of nestlings. It looks like they're going to do it again this year.

These birds need no birdhouse, but they do need water, so I've placed a birdbath just outside the deck and I keep it full of water. I can see Bird (as I've cleverly named him) and his mate bathing and splashing in it throughout the long days when they work so hard feeding the nestlings.

A birdbath is more than a decoration for the garden, it provides the essential element of water. Keep it clean by blasting it with the hose whenever you can. If there's water on your property, such as a small stream or a recirculating waterfall, you will probably still see birds at a birdbath. Since it's out in the open, the birds can keep an eye out for marauding cats or other predators. Birds like to perch on its lip, fluttering in and out of the shallow water.

Birds will certainly appreciate a well-stocked feeder, especially in winter, but remember that when you start feeding birds in winter, they will come to rely on the provisions you put out for them. If you suddenly stop feeding them, there is the chance that they will starve. Once you start feeding in winter, continue until well into spring.

Bird feeders can be simple affairs, but should stand up to invasion by squirrels, cats, and rats. There are various ways to make sure of this. Some feeders are made to tip squirrels off if they try to reach the food. Others have inverted skirts of barbed wire fixed to their poles,

One of the best ways to attract birds to your garden is with a birdbath. This classic example is in Wayne and Judy Gingrich's garden in White Rock, British Columbia. If there were a cat on the property, it would be best to keep the shrubs and foliage around the birdbath cut low, so the cat couldn't hide and pounce on an unsuspecting bather.

while still others may have an inverted metal box that the squirrels can't negotiate around. Really sharp-thorned rose canes tied in thick bundles around the pole will also deter raiders.

You can buy feeders that specifically attract different birds —a tube with thistle seed for finches, for instance, or a seed and suet cage for winter birds such as chickadees. The most common type of feeder is the flat bird table, which is both decorative and utilitarian. The ideal design has a roof that doesn't allow rainwater to leak on the table beneath it. A seed hopper into which the birds can peck is suspended from the roof. The table has edging or coping with gaps so it can be swept clean of old seed and debris; it is set on a smooth pole that cats can't climb, and fitted with a barrier to prevent squirrels and vermin from reaching the table.

Birdhouses and nesting boxes can help decorate the garden. Dovecotes and aviaries are the most elaborate kind of bird habitats for the garden. Dovecotes, essentially roosting places for cooing doves, can be built on top of conical roofs or be freestanding. Like birdhouses, they need to be placed atop the kind of slick metal poles cats can't climb. Aviaries are wire- or plastic-mesh enclosures in which birds are given perches and nesting places, but where they can fly free within the limits of the cage.

Purple martins and other social birds prefer "condominiums" on high poles out in the open, where they can swoop

Above: *The single red rose 'Dortmund' provides a beautiful setting for a round bird condominium in Orene Horton's garden in Columbia, South Carolina. 'Dortmund' is a* Rosa kordesii *hybrid introduced in Germany in 1955 and quite widely appreciated these days. The generously proportioned birdhouse with the charming perch supports, white finial, and fishscale shingled roof would be a magnificent decoration for any garden.*

Right: *The azaleas in the Steele family garden in Richmond, Virginia, provide hiding places, habitat, and food sources for birds that can then raise their families in the safety and comfort of the birdhouse raised above the bushes. This height allows birds to keep an eye out for cats. And the careful construction of the birdhouse enlivens the garden for its human inhabitants, too.*

Opposite: *A freestanding birdhouse accentuates the vertical elements in this passage at the home of Mr. and Mrs. Malcolm Buckenham at Brimscombe, Gloucestershire, England.*

in to land. These large houses are often quite elaborate, sometimes resembling Victorian homes with gingerbread peaks. Even simple birdhouses, however, enliven the garden.

Of all the birds to provide housing for, wrens are probably the best for insect control, for these voracious little eaters will consume their weight in insects every day—and then some. Not only that, but their busy comings and goings, their chatter, and the sound of their babies all bring cheer to the spring garden. Bluebird houses are a must, for if you're lucky enough to have a pair of eastern bluebirds nesting in your garden, you'll be rewarded with their lovely color and the sweetest birdsong there is.

Swallow nests can be mounted under the eaves of garden buildings, adding a decorative touch. Clay pots made from a design that dates back to colonial times are still being fashioned, and swallows will use these, especially when several are placed together under eaves. Keep sparrows out by hanging weighted strings six to eight inches in front of the holes. Sparrows won't like that but the swallows, which fly vertically up to their nests, won't mind.

Most cities have whole stores devoted to birdhouses and bird paraphernalia these days. You can find a range of decorative birdhouses there. Just make sure that your love of an elaborate house doesn't supersede care for the birds. A fancy birdhouse that allows cold rainwater to reach young nestlings is a cruel joke.

Right: Most bird feeders are utilitarian affairs, but this thatched-roof beauty in Ellen Coster's garden in Cutchogue, New York, is also decorative in a rustic way. A gorgeous Mandevilla × amoena *'Alice du Pont' is winding and flowering its way up to join the fun.*

Opposite: The birds who live in this charming house are fine, churchgoing folks, thanks to Sharon Abroms of Atlanta, who erected it in her garden. A Viburnum tinus *tosses its snowballs all around the birdhouse, and a specimen of lime green* Berberis thunbergii *'Aurea' lifts its gold leaves from below.*

....

Place all birdbaths, bird feeders, and birdhouses where cats can't get at them. Cat predation of songbirds, especially along the eastern United States flyways, is a serious problem. Belling the cats is not an answer, for young birds often have no idea that the tinkling of a bell means danger.

As you are cleaning up the garden, don't be quick to remove old stumps or dead trees. These become home to many species of insects and the birds that eat them. And don't remove all the weeds. A stand of local and native weeds is often a breeding place for beneficial insects that birds feed on.

Birds love the berries of many shrubs, especially Russian olive, cotoneasters, hollies, toyons, and viburnums. Seed-bearing umbelliferous plants like dill and fennel are especially valuable for their seeds as well as being host to many beneficial insects.

Among the best habitats for birds are thick stands of brambles such as wild blackberries. You don't want them taking over your property, but you might leave a stand for the birds. Blackberries also are home to many species of beneficial insects. What's more, you have the pleasure of berrying in July or early August.

◙ Toad Houses

Toads have great value in the garden, as they are voracious eaters of insects. Unlike frogs, they don't need a pond to live in. You may want to encourage your toads with a toad house.

Toad houses can be nothing more than a depression in the moist earth covered over with a capstone. But you might want something more decorative. Keep your eyes open for an ornamental roof, such as you might find on a ruined dollhouse, or that might be suggested by an old piece of metal you can spray with enamel paint.

Toads aren't particular about their houses. They just like a nice cool hole in the ground in which to hide for most of the day, so don't be too tricky here. It's fun to create something from found objects that covers the toad hole. It gives you the chance, when people ask you what it is, to tell them that it's a house for your favorite garden toads, and that the ones that are currently in disfavor will have to fend for themselves.

◙ Spirit Houses

Have you seen the Thai spirit houses? These elaborate, temple-like structures are about the size of a large martin house, and sit atop a pole in the garden. In Thailand they are erected as places for garden spirits to dwell. These spirits in

Left: *No Marie Antoinette in her milk bath bathed more beautifully than the sparrows who come to this lovely setting in Sarah Hammond's garden in Bolinas, California. The birdbath is surrounded by a thick, cat-hampering stand of* Lavandula angustifolia *'Martha Roderick'. The stones, mulched areas, and soft groundcovers make this twittery toilette something special.*

Opposite: *Two old-fashioned bee skeps, woven of reeds and prettily tied up with rushes, sit in front of pelargoniums on a rustic wooden bench in the Rancho Santa Fe, California, garden of Agatha Youngblood. Don't let bees nest in a skep, because the only way to harvest the honey from this device is to destroy the hive.*

turn keep things healthy and happy in the garden. If you find one, they make wonderful ornaments in any garden, and will be the talk of visitors for sure. But be aware that they are serious adjuncts to a religion, and not meant for fun.

Beehives

The coiled beehive that became the model for the beehive hairdo of the early 1960s is called a *skep*. It's a pretty, rustic, old-fashioned-looking thing, sitting atop its table in the garden. Have one if you must —but those who know bees abhor them.

The reason is that if bees actually take up residence in them, the only way to harvest their honey is to destroy the colony. Honeybees these days have a tough enough go of it; their numbers are dwindling due to mite infestations.

The invention of the beehive with removable frames was a great step forward from the skeps of the 18th century.

One can harvest honey from them without harming the bees, let alone destroying the colony.

If you want a skep for decorative purposes, close the hole with dark screening so that bees can't find their way in.

A modern beehive can be decorative and a source of honey, if you don't mind keeping bees. Site it where there's plenty of free space for the bees to take flight and land, and away from areas where children and garden visitors frequently walk. Bee colonies usually detail a couple of workers as guard bees. If you get too close to the hive, the guard bees may come out and sting you. The workers themselves are docile when working, and will usually only sting if they are hit.

A home orchard is a fine thing to have and a source of great pleasure as well as fruit. I've just returned from mine, where the apple trees are in full bloom, and a cloud of enticingly sweet yet faint fragrance is borne up on the balmy spring air. I think that the scent of apple blossoms must be the finest fragrance in the whole world. Your home orchard will be much more fruitful if there are bees nearby to work the trees and pollinate the blossoms.

CHAPTER NINE

For Kids of All Ages

The memories of childhood inspire our creation of gardens when we're adults. For this reason, it's important that as adults, we make sure there's a sense of fun and play in the garden, aimed to amuse and entertain children who use it and visit it.

The mistake often made is thinking that a garden alone is not enough to amuse and entertain children. Kids are often more adept than we grown-ups at finding unexpected sources of amusement. They will discover things about the garden that even we don't know: how a hydrangea leaf smells when it's rolled and crushed; how there's always a small black bug in the frilly center of each rose; what the inside of a lamb's ear leaf feels like; how the wild strawberries smell in June; what a mockingbird's song sounds like when you stick your fingers in and out of your ears really fast.

Adults can create gardens of classic beauty that will be appreciated differently by children. Kids will see a fort where we see a berm; they will see a place to lie spread-eagled under the sun where we see only an expanse of oxalis. The treasured viburnum whose spicy blossoms thrill us in spring becomes a place to hide and ambush an unwary brother or sister. Where we see a slope in need of ground cover, they see a hill down which to plunge willy-nilly, sword in hand, to attack the quiet cat.

These different points of view don't mean there can't be equipment in the garden that kids will like and use, but it does mean that for children, the best gardens are often the gardens adults like best. The gardener creates an imagined world when he creates a garden. For children, it's all an imagined world, and the adult's garden is a reality on which they project their play.

If you create a garden that's beautiful, you give children a model for beauty. It doesn't have to be an amusement park—the children will make it so. That said, you may still decide to put some play equipment into your landscape. I'd suggest you make a discrete area for this equipment, rather than space it through the garden. It will give the kids a place to play where they don't have to worry about running through a flower bed and trampling plants. It will also make the other areas of the garden more solemn and fun for them to explore carefully.

Play Equipment

Swings and Gliders

We've already mentioned Victorian swings in the section on garden furniture, but they are certainly beloved of children as well as romantically inclined adults. If kids are going to be using them, consider nailing a stop on the back so they can't be swung to the breaking point. As a child, I came precariously close to destroying more than one by testing its physics. The motion of gliders is usually self-limiting.

Swings are great fun and exercise for children, but for the adult who puts them up, safety should come first. Instead of hanging a swing from a tree limb—which can rub the bark off and damage the tree as well as pose safety problems—hang it from a metal crosspiece held up by braced triangles made of steel poles anchored in cement poured into the ground. Wobble is not tolerable, because it means eventual metal fatigue.

The swing seat can hang from chains, although there are stretchable rubber hangers available that allow kids to bounce as well as swing. The seat should be made of flexible, lightweight, woven nylon cord or rubber, rather than from a piece of metal or thick board, which can cause serious injury for a child who walks in front of it.

Even with a nylon or rubber seat, give the swing plenty of room in front and behind so that the child can swing high

and yet other children can safely pass by. And because children like to socialize in play areas, and you are already going to the trouble of making a sturdy frame, hang two or three swings together on the crosspiece. The distance from the center of one seat to the center of the next should be at least 4½ feet, preferably 5 (1.4–1.5 m).

Cable Railway

A woven wire cable is stretched taut between two trees, with one side slightly higher than the other. A trolley with handles on which a child (or childlike adult) can hang is suspended from the cable. The rider starts at the high end and zips swiftly down the cable to the

Opposite: *A colorful play set is given its own spot so that the kids don't damage plantings. Notice that the slide delivers the descending child to the soft grass. This installation is in a private garden in Spokane, Washington.*

Right: *A wheelbarrow bench resides in Bob Dash's garden in Sagaponack, New York. This is the ultimate in movable garden furniture. And you can line up the children on the bench and wheel them around the garden for some real fun.*

Below: *A miniature world in a shallow pot graces a table in Pat Welsh's garden in El Mar, California. The "ground" is covered with Corsican mint (*Mentha requienii), *while thyme, rosemary, and santolina form the trees and shrubs. Imagine the delight of any child (or adult who's still a child at heart) who discovers this treasure.*

Page 154: *A topiary gardener scampers, rake in hand, across Agatha Youngblood's garden in Rancho Santa Fe, California. The plant that covers the topiary shape is* Ficus pumila, *a vining plant whose leaves stay close to the surface they're growing on. While it is slow to get going, once established it will take off and cover large areas in a single season.*

other end. It's fun, and the garden is a good place to put it as long as there are no obstructions anywhere along the way.

Carousels and Seesaws

Carousels are circular platforms often found in schoolyards. They have sections where children can sit, and are suspended on a metal swivel in the center. Make sure there's plenty of room around them. Kids always try to see what kind of speed they can get out of the carousel, and centripetal force can send a child flying. If the child flies onto the grass, that's usually okay, but if there are trees within flight distance, you could have a bad accident. Carousels are available for home play. The sturdier the construction, the better.

Seesaws are always terrific fun, but remember that safety comes first. Place a seesaw where there's plenty of room around it. Kids need to see other children approaching, and kids running by need to see the seesaw in use to avoid getting hit when the high side descends. The word *seesaw*, by the way, comes from a reduplication of the word *saw*, and reflects the to-and-fro or up-and-down motion of men using a two-handled saw. Seesaws are usually found as complete kits, with the board held to a crosspiece by U bolts or O-type clamps. The legs of the crosspiece, like those of swing supports, should be set into concrete in the ground.

Slides

Of all outdoor play equipment, slides are probably the best loved by children. They involve daring, an uncontrolled ride, and a launch off into space at the bottom. Of course, as adults, we see that all this is gentle. But to a 3- or 4-year-old child, it's a challenge.

157

Your first consideration is safety. Make sure the slide is steady and anchored. Make sure the ground where the kids land is soft—use sand, if possible. Keep the slide part smooth and swift and free of dirt. A soft landing is important not only for slides but also under any climbing equipment (see page 185).

◙ Monkey Bars and Other Climbing Equipment

The soft safety surface described on page 185 should be installed under any climbing equipment, especially monkey bars. Although children can take a tumble from monkey bars, they are usually safer than trees, which seldom have soft surfaces underneath and often have dangerously placed or unstable limbs. I would never deny a child the experience of climbing trees, but having monkey bars at home may reduce the child's enthusiasm for tree climbing.

Monkey bars are fun. They should be made of metal to avoid splinters, but wooden ones are typically available for home installation. If the climbing frame is made of wood, make sure it's constructed of round poles of sufficient diameter to hold even the larger kids who'll use them to show off. These poles should be given several coats of glossy outdoor enamel paint.

Monkey bars with internal structure are preferable to a simple cage. As with other pieces of play equipment, the legs should be anchored in cement to avoid any wobble whatsoever.

Rope ladders are fun for children to

Froggy may have gone a-courtin', but it looks like he fell asleep among the ivy in Sally Cooper's garden in Charlotte, North Carolina. Children love surprises, of course, and it's the loving adult who hides unexpected touches of humor and whimsy for them, here and there.

climb. Try not to let them climb much higher than 6 or 7 feet (1.8–2.1 m), though. Even a simple rope suspended from a crosspiece can be climbed successfully by most children if double overhand knots are fixed into the rope every 2 or 3 feet (.6–.9 m).

Overhand bars help children develop a sense of rhythm as they exercise. A ladder with round wooden rungs will suffice if it's bolted securely to the top of a climbing frame. Make sure it's low enough for children to jump up and catch the rungs, but high enough for their legs to swing free when they do. Give them a lesson on how to swing one-handed from rung to rung, alternating hands with each rung, to move swiftly along the horizontal ladder. They'll soon be doing better than you.

◙ All-in-One Sets

High quality all-in-one play sets usually include monkey bars, a slide, a swing, sometimes an elevated platform or playhouse, and gymnastics-type rings. The latter require more muscle than most kids have, but they can be fun to hang from like a monkey. If you choose to install an all-in-one unit, buy the very best you can afford and give it a spot by itself, with no trees around. Build a board perimeter and fill the area with sand or shredded bark to soften falls.

◙ Game Courts

Most game courts are simply expanses of tough lawn grass surrounded by gardens. Here's where you play badminton, lawn bowling, croquet, soccer, and volleyball.

You can also think about working other kinds of dedicated game courts into your garden landscape. How wonderful to wander down a garden path flanked by

flowers to a bocce court, or a place for boules. Surely there's space somewhere for the iron pegs and ringing fun of horseshoes and quoits.

If you have lots of space and a level area, put in a basketball backboard and net, or even a place for softball. Tennis courts, of course, need a large dedicated space and plenty of resources for upkeep.

Tree Houses and Playhouses

The playhouse, along with its elevated counterpart the tree house, may be the ultimate garden accoutrement, magical and fantastic for children (see page 185). It is a symbol that the world is truly theirs, and doesn't belong exclusively to the adults. It is reassuring, too, as children comprehend that the adults have created something so absolutely marvelous just for them.

What kids don't know is that there are those moments when adults happily retreat to the tree house or playhouse to feel secure and private, and enjoy a moment's nostalgia for their own childhoods.

In the garden, the playhouse can be a very decorative feature. It should be given a spot where it's partially hidden by shrubs

Talk about a garden idea that will thrill the children! This train runs on time in Walt Nussbaum's garden in Savannah, Georgia. Holly, chamaecyparis, rosemary, camellias, and azaleas form the forests through which the train wends its merry way. The idea is a pure delight, but Walt had better bring his trains in before the rain arrives.

and small trees. Since it will be a hang-out for kids, site it away from the more formal gardens so their heavy foot traffic doesn't damage plantings. Enhance it with windowboxes and containers with a variety of flowering and trailing plants. Give it some touches that children will appreciate, such as a wooden shoe hung as a doorknocker, a piece of pipe painted with a checkerboard pattern for a chimney, or shutters with hearts cut out of their centers.

A tree house makes a fantastic and sought-after garden decoration. It is a very appealing sight, not just for children, but for adults as well. Use a paint in a natural color—sand, brown, green—to play off colors of native rocks and plants and to integrate it into the garden's scheme.

Other playhouses for children can be constructed of young willows planted very close together in a circle or in two opposing rows. As the willows grow, bend the tops of the saplings over and weave them together. They'll create a hut or tunnel of green that will offer children endless possibilities for play.

....

Left: *This very special garden playhouse, trimmed with rickrack and crowned with a lookout tower, was created by Angus White at Nuthurst in West Sussex, England. Pulleys allow the kids to haul booty of various kinds to the top floor; sturdy railings provide safety on all levels.*

Opposite: *A garden tree house offers an inviting vantage point for seeing the world below. This exciting one is in the Houston garden in Del Mar, California, built into a large specimen of* Schinus terebinthifolius.

CHAPTER TEN

Grottoes, Groves, and Hideaways

The idea of decorating a garden with ruins, with secret grottoes where sylvan nymphs played, and with sacred groves where Pan might be heard was a romantic notion that galvanized the gardening world in the 18th century. The notion of Arcadia as a rustic, pastoral paradise probably blossomed as the industrial revolution began to fill the air with soot, and the fields and milking herds of Constable were replaced by the smoky cities and engines of industry suggested by Turner.

While we've moved on into many new directions in gardening since then, the idea of ruins is still a strong one.

One of the first herb gardens I ever created was built in the ruins of a summer kitchen built in the late 18th or early 19th century in the farmlands of Palm, Pennsylvania. The building was about 15 by 20 feet (4.6 x 6.1 m), with a chimney at one end, and the walls were constructed of native stone, roughly dressed, fitted together with lime and horsehair mortar. The roof was of locally made terra-cotta tiles, like those that can still be seen on centuries-old buildings in the Pennsylvania Dutch counties.

When I moved to the property, the roof timbers had rotted and the roof had caved in. Rains had washed out the mortar from most of the top courses of the walls, and the stones had tumbled down. The chimney still stood, with some rusted iron hooks for hanging pigs and iron basins for rendering lard hidden under the rubble. Everything was covered with a mixture of weeds, briars, and the original old trumpet vines that had gone rampant and were doing a good job of pulling down whatever walls were left standing.

It took a couple of weeks of removing rubble to reveal the original cement-and-tile floor. I cleaned up the remaining walls and removed all the vegetation except the trumpet vine, which was given a shearing about 150 years overdue.

The resulting site was a delight, and I planted it with every herb I could think of—blue borage, nicotiana, oregano, mints, thymes, dittany, sages of all kinds, and much more. It was so nice that my wife and I were married there.

Nowadays people build ruined walls from scratch to evoke a site with a mood of antiquity and decay. I wouldn't go so far as to recommend building up something just to look destroyed, but the time-worn has a fascination, and if you have something old and ruined, made of natural materials, on your property, by all means take advantage of it.

A few old or truncated columns in the garden—not holding up anything, but just standing and looking as though they once were part of a temple—will express this mood beautifully for little effort.

▣ Grottoes

I speak about grottoes in the past tense because they seldom form part of modern gardens; yet, if you have the site, they are wonderful and spooky places to visit, and

the perfect setting for ferns and other shady plants that like water.

A grotto was a secret place in the earth—the kind of place that for the ancients was the abode of spirits and nymphs, and was held sacred. Usually there was a spring there, a source of water and thus of life itself. It was an opening into a netherworld from which this world issued. It resonated with the themes of birth and fecundity, and of the spirits of the dead as well.

The grotto itself was like a natural rock cave in a hillside, or an opening down to a spring. Inside it was cool and moist.

Perhaps there was a statue of a water god or goddess. How delightful if the ceiling of the grotto was pierced and a little top light came filtering down to glance off the water and make shimmering reflections on the rock walls and ceiling.

If the spring then flowed away into the surrounding woods, all the better, for there the ferns and brake would grow, and the watercress could be picked from the clean water, hovered over by tall, shaggy eupatoriums, with water irises splashing color here and there.

In our modern gardens, the grotto doesn't need water, but it surely must

Above: *A formal stone grotto fills the space beneath the stairs above it. It's been crafted to have the look and feeling of an ancient place, although Prince Wolkonsky built it recently at Kerdalo, his garden in Treguier, France.*

Opposite: *A castlelike stone facade is approached by a diamond-stepped pathway at Kerdalo. Inside the grotto water, the universal symbol of life, pours from a wall, as the spark of life is hidden within the human frame. Thus the grotto becomes a symbol of the place where life springs up, the source, the holy of holies.*

Page 162: *Surely this French grotto, guarded by a brilliant azalea and crowned with ivy, is home to some sprite or other. Europeans, with their long history stretching back to pagan times and beyond, know more about garden grottoes than Americans, who so recently wrested their landscape from raw nature. This prime example of a grotto is found at Château de Nacqueville in Cherbourg, Normandy.*

give a feeling of penetrating back into an earthen bank, with natural rock enclosing it. Statues can still be found there—perhaps nowadays the ubiquitous serving girl with her water jug, or a Virgin Mary with outstretched palms.

If you have a steep bank with large stones or rock, you could chisel out a grotto with a floor deeper than ground level, install a recirculating pool, and hide the return hose behind rocks in the back of the grotto, so that water trickles down stone there. It would be an elaborate construction, though; perhaps you'd do better to scout the property for the makings of a grotto—a natural seep or spring, a bank where stones already form the opening. If the grotto is grafted onto a suburban lot, it probably won't be worth the effort, but if it can be created on an arcadian country property that some nature spirits may still call home, it makes a strong feature.

Groves

A grove of trees—especially trees planted in a circle with an empty center—was often sacred to the ancients. Druid priests had certain magical trees that they used to plant, among them rowan (European mountain ash or *Sorbus aucuparia*), yew, oak, maple, and larch.

A pretty grove of trees is still an appealing feature in a garden, even if you don't believe in its magical properties. The shade is cooling, and one can plant shade-tolerant grasses in the center so there's a place for the picnic blanket, a bench, or a picnic table.

Site your grove in an out-of-the-way place. You want it to have a quiet and secluded feeling. Choose trees that mean something to you, the way you might select charms for a charm bracelet. But make them compatible—that is, choose trees that will reach about the same size when mature, and site them accordingly. The best are those, like the rowan, that reach perhaps only 20 feet (6.1 m) or so when fully grown. No matter which trees interest you, there are usually small or semidwarf species or cultivars available. In a sunny location, fruit trees are nice both when they are in bloom and in fruit. In a more closed-in, shady spot such as mixed woodlands, most trees will respond to shade down below by growing taller to reach the sun.

Be aware that some shade trees are understory trees—amelanchier, pepperwood, and clethra, for instance—that will not grow tall and prefer to grow under the canopies of the large trees.

Plant the large trees in a circle so

sonal meaning for you—I personally might want a purple smoke bush (*Cotinus coggygria*), a black currant bush, and a 'Gruss an Aachen' rose because of my personal associations with these plants.

If you make a hideaway, keep it small, or everyone will find it. Fashion it so no one can see in, but you can see out. Decorate it with things you personally love. It's for you. Only you will know what these things are.

I once had a hideaway that I used to visit as soon as I came home from high school. I didn't construct it, but I knew where it was. Through some woods and down a north slope to a stream, there was a shady bank with a curled root that rushing waters had exposed. I stashed a bottle of soda pop in the cold stream

that there's a space 30 feet (9.2 m) across within. As they grow, their branches will touch, forcing them to grow upward and eventually forming a canopy over the center, through which some sunbeams will slant to the grove floor.

You might plant shade-tolerant evergreen shrubs such as holly or pittosporum between the trees for privacy, or just for the decorative look of them. You can also use understory trees and shrubs like rhododendrons to flank the tall trees.

Since the grove is intended to be a place of refuge, keep furniture to a minimum, but you might want to place a bench there for comfortable seating or a table for picnics.

You might also plant a group of trees randomly so they make a natural grove, without an open center or geometric planting pattern. This will create a naturalistic effect, as though nature had done the planting, and still give you a closed-in, private, quiet place to repair to when the world is too intrusive.

Hideaways

How fortunate those gardeners who have room to construct a hideaway on their property! A hideaway can be any place that makes a little secret garden—like the children's tale.

It can be hidden by fencing, shrubbery, trees, stones, or hedging. Few should know about it. You can plant it with plants you care about and that have per-

Above: *An out-of-the-way spot becomes a private reading nook in Jody Honnen's garden in Rancho Santa Fe, California. The lavender flowers of* Alyogyne huegelii *decorate the spot, which is protected by a large specimen of* Melaleuca linariifolia, *with its interesting bark that peels off in papery layers.*

Opposite: *Gardens are a refuge for the world-weary, refreshing us, cheering us, and giving us solace. Here at Gordon Hayward's garden in Putney, Vermont, a pathway enticingly lined with* Nepeta x faassenii *'Six Hills Giant' leads to a rustic structure recalling druidic rites—or perhaps just the underpinnings for a soothing arbor of vines that may grow along the poles.*

each day, and pulled out the one I had put there the day before. I'd hidden a bottle opener in a curve of the tree root, and the stream water made a splashing sound as it came over some rocks on its way to the little village a couple of miles away. Sitting back in the curl of the big root, I felt like I was visiting a friend, and I'd drink the cold soda with relish and notice all of nature easily going about her business—the dragonfly, the bird in the tree, the stream with its minnows, and the vegetation soaking up the buttery sunlight in the field beyond.

I savored the half-hour or so I'd spend, sitting by the stream in midafternoon, letting the tension drain away with the water that flowed away down the stream. In every garden I've made since, I have found a place that's my hideaway, but I've never found one quite as satisfying as that one by Kettle Creek, in the woods alongside Paul Harps's cow pasture, in the mountains of my boyhood. I suspect I never will.

Projects

Berm (see pages 14–17)

Gardeners have several tricks for hiding unpleasant sights on the property, and putting in a berm is one of them. A propane tank, never attractive, may mean the difference in the kitchen between the joy of cooking with gas or the aggravation of cooking with electricity. One way to hide it from view is to place it by the house and then mound earth in a berm between the tank and the rest of the garden. If the berm is then well planted, the tank should be invisible. The alternatives are usually more expensive, and seldom become an integral part of the landscape the way a berm does.

Creating a berm gives the gardener an opportunity to bury electrical cables or water pipes in the safe center of the berm,

---

A yew fence has a window trimmed into it, through which we see bright geraniums blooming. This tricky and effective decorative touch is in the Upton Wold garden of Mr. and Mrs. I.R.S. Bond, Moreton-in-Marsh, Gloucestershire, England.

where subsequent digging will not be likely to damage them. I've buried pipes in the lawn, and then over time have forgotten exactly where the pipes are. It's an unpleasant surprise to dig into irrigation pipes or hit electrical wiring. By placing these at the center bottom of a berm, you will always remember exactly where they are, minimizing the risk of poking into them as you garden.

If your yard is rectangular, a berm that sweeps around the perimeter in a graceful arch (with the farthest point of the arch at the middle of the far boundary) will add a very natural feeling. The far corners of the yard, beyond the berm, now become triangular areas, just right for planting large, dark evergreens as background plants for lighter, more colorful foreground plants on the berm itself.

You might consider filling the triangular corners behind the berm with soil, raising the corners of the yard to the level of the berm, and transforming the berm in those corners into a bank. On flat terrain, however, doing so may mean constructing a wall along the property line to hold in the raised portion. Visually, the berm accomplishes much of the same effect as

the bank, only without all the added soil and retaining wall.

To situate a berm, stand where you most frequently walk out from the house and envision the yard rising in a gentle slope, turning the yard into a partial bowl. Always remember that such a bowl will trap water. Unless you plan to add a pond with an outlet, make sure the water can run or drain off the yard easily. If water consistently ponds in low spots, drowning plants and lawn grass and making an unsightly spot, you may need to install french drains.

A french drain carries excess water away underground, and it is easier to build than you'd imagine. Dig a trench about 18 inches (46 cm) wide and 1 foot (30 cm) deep where you want the water to flow. Place a couple of inches of pea gravel in the bottom, then lay perforated pipe, which is sold at most building supply stores, along the length of the trench, with the far end of the pipe, where the water will exit, placed in a drainage ditch or spot where the water can freely flow away. Take a long length of roofing paper about a foot wide, creased down the center, and lay it over the top of the pipe. The paper keeps soil that washes down into the french drain from clogging up the small slits in the perforated pipe.

Now fill the trench to the top with gravel or cobbles. When water runs down to the place where the drain is laid, it will easily seep through the gravel and enter the perforated pipe, which will carry it away. It performs well, and yet the gravel that you see is not unattractive, and you can walk on it.

PROJECT TWO

River of Stones (see pages 29–30)

Once you've determined where the river should go, smooth the course by removing any existing stones, twigs, roots, and plants; you may choose to leave any grass, and simply smother it. The next step is to lay down where the course is to run some 30-mil black plastic sheeting such as EPDM (ethylene propylene diene monomer). Remember to give your river meanders, or graceful back-and-forth curves, through the property.

Now cover the black plastic with coarse sand, and then add pebbles and some cobbles to the outer edges, working toward the center with bigger rounded stones. Stones become round or smooth-edged by eons of wear by water, so using water-smoothed stone adds to the effect. A river of sharp-edged stones is just going to look like a rock pile.

The majority of the largest stones should lie at the very center of the channel,

Stones of varying size half buried in sand give a very natural look to a river of stones that courses through a garden of succulents and sword-leaved phormiums in San Marcos, California. The river of stones has a practical purpose as well as a decorative one. The stones slow the movement of water from torrential winter rains that would erode unprotected soil.

....

although your river will look most natural when the stones aren't noticeably demarcated. Mix some small stones and sand with the large stones in the center, and allow a few large stones to reach the edges of the river.

You can then sink large pots or half barrels here and there in the stone course by pushing the stones out of the way, cutting out the plastic, and burying the pot or barrel close to the edge of the rim. You can fill these with water and sink a pot of water lilies under the water, and use goldfish to

keep mosquitoes down, as the fish will gobble up any larvae that hatch. Or sink a pot of rushes or water grass under the water. On the grassy bank where the river of stones meets the lawn or garden, use plants with a fountain-shaped habit, like Buddleia alternifolia or Miscanthus sinensis, to spray out and arch over and down to the stones, hiding the edge of the stone course in several places.

PROJECT THREE

Winter Handling of Tropical Water Lilies

(see page 36)

For overwintering, pull up the plants in their pots and remove them to a work area, after the first frost or two, or when the temperature of the water in your lily pond goes down to 50 degrees Fahrenheit (10°C). Cut off leaves and flower stems. Then remove the plant gently from the pot. Cut off any remaining stems, then wash off as much soil as you can. Look beneath the crown for tubers the size of the joint on your thumb closest to your wrist. These are generally black, and will become next year's lilies. Gently separate them from the old crown, then place them in lukewarm water. The viable ones will sink, and any duds will float. Discard the duds.

After soaking the tubers in water for a day or so, dry them on newspapers for a few days in a basement or cool room; alternatively, you can leave them in cold water for a couple of weeks, rinsing them every day.

Now fill a porous sack, such as a pillowcase, with sand and thoroughly wet the sand, then let it drain for a day. Now put a big scoop—about 4 cups—of the drained, damp sand in a plastic bag, bury a tuber in the sand, twist-tie the bag, and store your collection of bags in a cool, dark place—preferably a basement where the temperature stays about 50 degrees. Just don't let them freeze.

About 4 weeks before your last frost date, check the tubers. Place any that haven't started sprouting in some water on a warm, sunny windowsill. Get the tubers going by potting them up in small (4-inch or 10 cm) pots filled with good garden soil so that their crowns are just at soil level. Add pebbles so the soil doesn't float away, and sink the pots a few inches under water in a tub or pail or aquarium. Keep the water temperature at about 70 degrees Fahrenheit (20°C). A heating cable of the kind used under seed trays is good, or use an aquarium heater. When you see a nice tuft of new leaves, move the water tubs with the plants in them into as bright and sunny a spot as you have.

When your outdoor pool temperature reaches 70 degrees, repot the sprouted tubers into large (5-gallon or 19 l) pots. Don't hurry this step, as cold water will set the plants back and you'll lose weeks of bloom time. Keep the crowns at soil level. Cover the soil with pebbles, leaving the crowns and tufts of leaves exposed. Sub-merge the pots in your lily pond so the crowns are about 6 to 8 inches (15–20 cm) under the surface for a long season of bloom.

PROJECT FOUR

In-Ground Lily Pond

(see pages 36–39)

There are three basic ways to construct your lily pond. Each of these options has its pros and cons.

The pond can be made of concrete, but this method is expensive and should be done by a professional. The concrete will need reinforcing steel. The pond will need positive winter maintenance so if it freezes, the ice won't break up the concrete. Repairs to concrete pools are expensive.

You can also construct the pond using a rigid, preformed pool liner. These come in various amorphous and regular shapes and are usually fairly shallow. You must dig a hole for the liner so it fits snugly, otherwise torque and tension on unsupported parts can twist and break the rigid liner. Should the liner break, repairs are difficult and expensive. Usually these liners are made of plastic that can eventually break down after prolonged exposure to sun and can also become brittle and break because of ice pressure. Liners are also available in more durable fiberglass, although they are more expensive than plastic.

Flexible pool liners are the option I prefer. They can be folded to fit any size hole you dig for the pond. (Just don't try to use the thin polyethylene sheeting they sell at the hardware stores, which will crack and degrade in just a few years.) There are thicker types of polyethylene, but other materials have its advantages without its drawbacks—mostly its stiffness and difficulty to work with. Polyvinyl chloride (PVC) liners are one option. They come in large sheets 32 mil thick, and they are adequate for most lily pond uses; in cold-winter areas, however, PVC becomes brittle and stiff and cracks easily. In the past, butyl rubber sheets were used in such

Joanna Reed's gorgeous stone farmhouse in Malvern, Pennsylvania, needs a lily pond worthy of its beauty, and that's what it gets with this stone and mortar circular pond out among the perennials in her back yard. The stone frog and inviting pads of the nymphaea surely encourage real frogs to add their music to the pond at night.

cold areas, because the rubber stayed flexible in cold weather. These sheets have been superseded by EPDM—ethylene propylene diene monomer. It's black, flexible, nontoxic, easy to work with and repair, comes in the thicknesses required by pools (at least 30 mils), and will be durable for many, many years. Most pool contractors will recommend it.

When constructing the pond, dig out the hole at three levels, each of which can encircle the whole pool. The first level is just 6 inches (15 cm) down from the soil surface. The pool liner will be folded and laid on this shelf, then stones placed on the folded liner so it can't be seen after the pond is filled. If you choose to put in a second shelf, construct it 18 inches (46 cm) below the first (24 inches [61 cm] below the soil surface). The very bottom of the hole will then be another 18 inches below that.

It's very important to remove any rocks and broken roots from the hole, as they can rupture the liner when it is filled with the considerable weight of the water. Most pool makers line the bottom of the hole with sand and smooth the sides, or line the whole pit with a woven geotextile fabric such as woven polyethylene or the soil cloth used as a weed barrier. These prevent punctures. Then the actual liner is laid in the hole and carefully folded vertically to keep excess material as low-profile as possible. Try to make the liner surface as smooth as possible stretching it out; when excess material accumulates, fold it under itself up along the sides and onto the 6-inch shelf. Keep folding and stretching until the entire hole is lined.

PROJECT FIVE

Edging for a Pool

(see pages 36–39)

If your lily pond is going to be completely still, then you don't have to worry about burying conduit for an electrical connection for a recirculating pump and/or filter system. If you do plan to recirculate the water for a waterfall, or for filtration in such a way that the lilies aren't disturbed, such as by growing the lilies in a quiet backwater or eddy, then bring your conduit to the pond through a trench sunk 6-inches (15 cm) below the lawn or garden surface, so that it emerges at the level of the 6-inch-deep shelf. From there you can use submersible wiring to the submersible pump. Remember that lilies don't like moving water, so a lily pond is not the place for a fountain or a waterfall.

The pool liner is now folded neatly around the edge of the pool, tucked down on the 6-inch shelf. The next step is to rim the shelf with stones so they cover the edge of the folded liner. Because the shelf is usually a constant 6 inches wide all around the top rim of the pool, the temptation is to use stones of all one size and place them side by side—dink, dink, dink—around the rim. This looks contrived and artificial to me, although you see it often enough.

I prefer a more naturalistic appearance, where the pool looks like an integral part of the landscape, as if it had naturally formed there. This is the most aesthetically pleasing and restful-looking way to decorate the edge of your pond.

Start by choosing the largest stone available—something it may take two people to move. Dig out the back of the 6-inch shelf into the lawn, or garden, to accommodate the large stone. This large stone will thus be set 6 inches down into the soil, and will cover the folded liner, and perhaps protrude an inch or so out over the water. Set the stone at a diagonal to the pool's long horizontal axis, rather than parallel or perpendicular to it.

For an added naturalistic effect, you might dig back into the lawn deeper than the 6-inch shelf so that the stone tilts on its vertical axis, with the end toward the lawn more deeply buried than the end toward the water, and the higher end of the stone arising from the ground.

Once you have this largest, main stone in place, you can key all the other stones to it. Consider its long axis to be the direction that the bedrock has fractured. Most of the other stones should be positioned to more or less follow along in loose parallel. Too much precision in the form of exact parallel placement looks forced.

The next two largest stones should be close together—even touching, slightly away from exactly across the pool from the main stone. Make sure that one of them is fairly parallel to the main stone, and the other slightly askew from parallel. Another stone, slightly smaller than the last two, should now go near the main stone, on the other side of the pool from the last two. After that, choose and use stones of smaller sizes as you see fit. You may want one large

The color of the stones used for this pond in Southampton, New York, is reflected in the seedheads of the fountain grass (Pennisetum alopecuroides) and in the revealed branching of the tree in the background. Juniperus 'Blue Pacific' reflects the blue of the sky and the water.

flat stone right where people will walk up to the pool, so they can stand on it. You'll find your cats will sit on this stone when they come to drink from your pool and eye your goldfish. While most cats won't fish out your goldfish, raccoons will. The best defense against marauding raccoons is a dog with the run of the property at night.

If your pool is built into the bottom of a slope, the very back of the pool, into the slope, is a fine place for the largest stone. It looks natural there, and can be buried in the slope to suggest that it is being exposed by years of rains that have washed soil away

from it. The lily pool will also look natural in that position, as though the big rock shelters a secret spring that forms the pool. When constructing this arrangement, extend your pool liner into the area excavated for the big stone and slightly up the bank. Then set your large stone in place so that its bottom sits on pool liner and its back is against 12 to 18 inches (31–46 cm) of pool liner on the face of the slope. The liner helps prevent rain from loosening the soil behind and under the stone. If the shelf and bank become too saturated, the edge of the pool may crumble and dump stone and mud into the pool. With the liner behind and under the stone, rain falling there will run on the liner into the pool, and the soil under the heavy stone won't become loose.

With the pool edge rocked in, backfill any disturbed earth on the lawn or garden side with compost and sow grass seed, ground cover, or whatever you wish there. It won't be long before the plants grow up to and around parts of the stones, giving a very natural appearance to the pool.

PROJECT SIX

Wishing Well (see page 44)

To install a wishing well, first find a spring by observing where water comes to the surface, and dig down far enough that you reach water of 2 or 3 feet (.6–.9 m) deep (no deeper, or the well becomes a hazard for children and animals). This is deep

enough for your bucket to enter and fill. Make sure that water constantly seeps or runs in and leaves through an underground channel. This will keep the water clear. Have the water tested for purity. Springs are often pure enough to drink, and there's nothing like a cold draft of real springwater after a work session in the garden.

Once you've excavated the hole for the spring, line the sides with brick, stones, or cinder blocks up to ground level. Turn bricks sideways here and there so they protrude 6 inches (15 cm) into the cavity, forming a ladder out for any cats or other animals that might tumble in. At ground level, you'll want to excavate a footer, fill it with concrete, and build a circular wall of brick or stone and mortar 3 or 4 feet (.9–1.2 m) high.

Leave holes for square metal sockets on each side of the wall and cement them in place. Use upright timbers (4-by-4s or larger), drill holes to accept a 2-inch (5 cm) diameter crank, and build a roof supported by bracing from the upright timbers. The crank is wrapped with rope attached to a bucket, and when the bucket is up, fix a stop on the side of the timber that can be turned out to engage the crank handle and prevent it from turning.

PROJECT SEVEN

Waterfall (see pages 44–46)

When assessing your property for a place to site a waterfall, look first to your slopes,

A series of waterfalls pouring into a swimming pool will attract avian bathers, while human ones are soothed by the musical splash of water and the visually arresting composition.

and then decide where water would naturally run if a small stream came through the area.

Now make a pool, using a flexible liner and recirculating pump as described in chapter 2 and in Projects Four and Five. Site the pool at the bottom of the slope. Dig out enough of the slope so that there's a flat shelf of earth on the slope side of the pool before the slope begins to climb upward. Place the liner so there's extra liner laid up against the bank or slope, about as high as your rocks for the waterfall will go.

If the pool is relatively small and water volume isn't more than 5 gallons

(19 l) a minute, use a length of clipped garden hose; place one end in the pool and bring it up the slope, laying it against the liner, so it reaches a few feet higher than the spot where your rocks will end. If your system requires a larger pump, you may want to use 1½-inch (3.8 cm) flexible pipe to carry the water from the pond to the top of the waterfall.

Using native stone, if possible (or at least stone of all one type and color), place your stones around the pool and back up the slope in as naturalistic a manner as possible. This means fitting some in front of others, rather than simply stacking them on top of one another. Extend the rocks past the side and top edges of the liner and put plants such as ferns and sedums between the rocks so they begin to grow into the part of the rocks backed by liner.

Try to keep the lip stones (protruding rocks that act as a spout for the waterfall) at the level of the water behind them to prevent deep pools from forming. The water flowing downhill should be no more than 3 inches (7.6 cm) deep. Keep in mind that the water will splash musically if it drops off the lip of a protruding rock down to one below. You can create pools coming down the slope with waterfalls at the lips of each, or have just one fall. A cascade from the lip of one rock onto a larger one below will also become a favorite bathing place for birds. They'll flit in, splash about on the lower rock, shake their feathers, take a drink, and fly off.

Once you've finished placing your rocks, cut the hose or pipe where you want the water to flow out at the top, making

sure that all the water will spill into an area lined with the flexible liner. If water seeps behind the liner, it can soften and weaken the bank, and your whole construction may end up in the pool of water at the bottom.

Place rocks and stone at the end of the pipe to slow the water before it flows out from the rocks and begins its journey down the slope to the fall and the pool below.

PROJECT EIGHT

Millstone Fountain
(see page 51)

Old millstones come ready-made with holes in the center; the scored striations on the surface, originally designed to carry the flour off the stone, will just as easily carry water in streaming channels.

A good way to handle a millstone fountain is to sink in the ground a large, waterproof holding tank, at least 3 feet (1 m) larger in diameter than the millstone. Place a recirculating pump connected to buried electrical service in the center bottom of the tank; then use bricks or cinder blocks to build three strong piers radiating out at 120 degree angles from each other and reaching to ground level. The horizontal millstone will rest on these piers. As the millstone is lowered into place, insert a pipe from the water pump into the bottom of the hole on the millstone. The millstone then comes to rest on the three piers so that its bottom face is at ground level and its entire width rises above ground level.

Now place large cobbles into the space between the edge of the tank and the piers so that they fill the space solidly up to about 1 foot (31 cm) below ground level. Next, fill the top foot of space with small cobbles. The tank is then filled with water, which should not rise quite to the level of the cobble surface.

Excavate a space 1 foot or so wide and 1½ feet (46 cm) deep just outside the tank—or if it's been excavated before the tank was set in, it should be back-filled to within 1½ feet of ground level. Add soil mixed with compost to within a few inches of ground level and place there some plants that will spread out in both directions, spilling onto

....

A millstone used as the centerpiece of a fountain spreads a shimmering disk of water that drains into a catch basin below the stones and is recirculated up through the center of the millstone. The effect is riveting.

the small cobbles by the millstone and outward toward the lawn or garden.

Now more of the same small cobbles should be placed over the soil surface of this outer cobbled ring so that they make a seamless surface from lawn or garden right to the millstone, hiding the lip of the tank.

When the electricity is turned on, the pump will force water up so it bubbles out over the millstone. If the stone is perfectly flat, it will run off in all directions, then down through the cobbles into the buried tank and through the piers to the pump, to be recirculated back up the pipe to the millstone.

If dealing with a heavy millstone is beyond your ambition, you can create a circular cobbled area, slightly depressed in the center, that leaves out the millstone and allows the water to come bubbling up out of the ground like an artesian fountain. No one but you need know that it runs down through the cobbles into a holding tank where it's recirculated back up to the surface.

PROJECT NINE

Bog Garden (see page 53)

If you have plenty of scraps of EPDM flexible pool liner left over from other projects, use them for a boggy garden. If not, you might buy more, or something less expensive, such as 30-mil PVC liner.

Excavate the area of your bog garden

to a depth of about 18 inches (46 cm). Put down tarps to hold the excavated soil just a few feet away, as you'll have to return this soil to the excavation. You can make the excavation any size, but remember that if you make it wider than you can reach from the margins, you may have to put in stepping stones so you can get into the center to weed and work the garden. A compact, free-form area about 5 feet by 15 feet gives you 75 square feet of bog to plant (1.5 x 4.6 m = 6.9 m²).

Once the area is excavated, make a shelf around the rim 4 inches (10 cm) deep. Place the liner or overlapping pieces of liner in the hole so that their edges come up and rest on the shelf. The idea here is to slow down the rate of percolation, not necessarily to stop it entirely. So if you're using a single sheet of liner, you should make a half dozen 6-inch (15 cm) slits here and there over the bottom surface that lines the excavation.

As you replace the soil, apportion two parts of soil to one part compost or enriched organic soil. Bogs generally have lots of wet, decaying organic matter and consequently low pHs. Finish the bog area by making a low, raised berm over the shelf where the edges of the flexible liner are buried. This berm doesn't have to be wider than 8 inches (20 cm) or so, and should be low and rounded, not steep-sided. You can then plant the edges of the bog with grasses and other plants that like drier conditions, making a transitional area on the low berm.

If there is adequate rainfall in your area, you may not need to water. But if things get dry, a good sprinkling will soon

Some Useful Plants for the Bog Garden

SHRUBS

Amelanchier *spp.*, *serviceberry*

Calluna vulgaris, *heather*

Clethra alnifolia, *sweet pepperbush*

Halesia carolina, *Carolina silverbell*

Rhododendron viscosum, *swamp azalea*

Rosa pulstris, *swamp rose*

Vaccinium macrocarpon, *cranberry*

PERENNIALS

Althaea officinalis, *marshmallow*

Asclepias incarnata, *swamp milkweed*

Caltha palustris, *marsh marigold*

Eupatorium maculatum *'Gateway'*,
    Joe Pye Weed

Filipendula rubra *'Venusta'*, *meadow-
    sweet*

Gentiana septemfida *var.* lagodechiana,
    gentian

Geranium macrorrhizum *'Ingwersen's
    Variety'*, *hardy geranium*

Hibiscus moscheutos *'Lord Baltimore'*,
    rose mallow

Iris ensata, *Japanese iris*

Iris pseudacorus, *yellow flag*

Lobelia cardinalis, *cardinal flower*

Lysimachia clethroides, *gooseneck
    loosestrife*

Myosotis scorpioides *'Semperflorens'*,
    forget-me-not

Trollius chinensis *'Golden Queen'*,
    globeflower

Veronicastrum virginicum *'Album'*,
    Culver's root

Zantedeschia aethiopica, *calla lily*

Small lavender Myosotis, the grass mounds of miscanthus, hostas, and the true water plant, Eichhornia crassipes, blooming as it floats, decorate this small pond in Ellen Coster's garden, designed by Connie Cross, in Cutchogue, New York.

Invasive Plants to Avoid

These water-loving plants will take over your bog garden if you allow them in, so it's best to avoid them.

Mentha aquatica, *water mint*

Typha *spp.*, *cattail*

Houttuynia cordata, *chameleon plant*

Equisetum *spp.*, *horsetail*

saturate the bog garden. Set a few glasses here and there and turn on the sprinkler. When the glasses have 2 to 3 inches (5–8 cm) of water in them, that should be plenty. Since the liner will prevent water from percolating out, you'll need to water the bog garden much less frequently than the better-drained parts of the property.

PROJECT TEN

Dry Wall and Freestanding Wall

(see pages 57–59)

Master wall builders seat stones by tossing or dropping them in place. If you try to set a stone in place with your hands, you'll undoubtedly squish more than a few fingers. Rather, hold the stone above the spot and then let it drop in.

Because natural stone comes in a variety of irregular sizes and shapes, building a wall with it is not like laying a brick wall. You usually have to try several stones in a space to get the right one, and then you have to turn it this way and that until it magically lands with a satisfying thunk. You'll notice when you push it that it moves only a little, if at all. Building a dry wall of native stones provides a continuing series of little triumphs as each stone finds the place in the wall that it was made for. When a stone is right, it sounds right going in, it feels sturdy when it is in, and it looks great in the spot.

Before we go further with the fun of placing stones, however, we have to make sure that our dry wall has the proper foundation, and that drainage has been taken into account.

Because water expands when it freezes, the dry wall will be much more stable over time if you create a foundation footer that wicks water away. Dig a trench about 6 to 18 inches deep (15–46 cm) and as wide as the course of stones. In the warmer zones, 6 inches will be sufficient. In the colder northern tier of states, 18 inches is best. In the very coldest areas, you might need to go deeper than that to prevent frost heaving.

If the wall will hold a bank, place the trench at the bottom of the bank. Smooth the bottom of the trench so that the foundation stones—your largest—fit snugly down in the trench. If the wall turns a corner, place your largest stone at the corner. This stone should be as deep as the wall is wide.

Leave a few inches of space between the foundation stones, and when this first course is entirely laid, fill in the space with pea gravel. Any rainwater that runs into the interior of the wall and makes its way to the foundation will be carried down to the subsoil and percolate away. The pea gravel helps water run down and away, and the spaces between foundation stones allow for movement when the inevitable frosts do torque and heave the soil.

Make sure that water won't pond against the subsoil, but can drain easily away. By sloping the trench just slightly to one end, rainwater will drain off at the lower end. The wall can still be level at its top by building it just slightly higher at the lower end.

In my case, where two huge anchor stones were already in place (courtesy of Mother Nature), I dug the footer up to one of the anchor stones, then continued it on the other side to the next boulder. Although my anchor stones were already in place, that probably won't be the case for you. You'll need a very large anchor stone at least every 12 feet (3.7 m), and especially at the base of a corner if your dry wall makes a bend, as noted above.

A freestanding dry wall will need a slightly different kind of footer. Dig out a trench about 1 foot deep (31 cm) and as wide as the wall will be at its base. Now snug the base stones down into the smooth-bottomed trench, again leaving space between these foundation stones and filling the space with gravel, and build from there.

Not every large rock need go at the base, although most of them should. Walls look good when a few large stones are built up in the face, too.

Before you begin to lay stone for a dry retaining wall, make sure that the bank behind the wall slopes backward slightly. If you have a lot of water coming down the hill above the bank during rains, you may want to fill the space between the bottom course of stones and the bank face with a french drain and a layer of pea gravel, so that water behind the wall is also carried away; if it ponds up it may expand in freezes and push the wall out.

The wall itself will be built to lean against this sloping bank, or "batter." As you set each stone in place, tip it slightly so its back end—the part extending back toward or into the bank—is lower than the exposed front. Though the exposed face of the wall may look perpendicular, a side view of the wall will show it leaning slightly back toward the bank, and the unseen back of the wall built back against the slope. This means that the weight of the wall is resting against both the footer and the bank face—a much more stable arrangement than if all the weight is on the footer and foundation stones. It also means that the pressure of expanding frozen soil, or soil moving naturally down the slope behind the wall, will not as easily be able to push out the wall. Properly built this way, a dry wall should be able to stand for millenia—as Roman dry walls in Britain and ancient walls from Mycenae to Machu Picchu attest.

Whether building a retaining or freestanding wall, use the two-over-one, one-over-two technique, in which the joint between any two rocks on a course is covered by a stone on the course above. If all the abutments in a wall are directly over one another, the joints will run from the base to the top, forming a split or run, which is inherently unstable. But when a stone covers the joint below, and joints above are sitting on a length of stone below, there's much less chance of slippages or failure in the wall.

Use headers every 3 feet (1 m) or so in every course, and especially at corners or sharp bends. A header, also called a bind stone or a tie stone, is a stone that extends from the face of the wall all the way through to the other side of the freestanding wall or to the bank behind. Often you will need two stones to extend the full width of the wall. The prettiest stone, of course, will be on the exposed face, but the one behind it—although unseen—will still be needed as part of the wall's structure. Just make sure that at least every 3 feet (1m) on every course, a stone large enough to reach from the face to the bank is used.

As you add stones, use small pieces of roughly hewn stone to fill in chinks, help stabilize the larger stones around them, and prevent empty chambers in the wall where animals like chipmunks, wood rats, and even groundhogs will hide, and from which they will forage to prey on your garden. Speaking of groundhogs, these burrowing creatures don't usually live in chambers up in the wall, but prefer a burrow under it, and these burrows can be quite devastating. As the groundhog excavates soil under the wall, something will eventually give and cave in—and that will be your carefully laid stone. Once that happens, instabilities are opened in the wall and it will turn to rubble. So keep the groundhogs away from your garden walls any way you can.

When building a freestanding dry wall, make sure both faces have a good batter, with the wall receding about an inch for every foot of rise (or a centimeter for every 12 centimeters of rise). A 3-foot wall is thus 3 inches narrower at the top than the bottom.

A freestanding wall should be built so that the ends of the stones in the wall's interior are slightly lower than the exposed faces. This inverted spine assures that both faces of stone lean back toward each other,

A well-made dry wall of carefully selected stones forms a terrace with an inviting seat made of cemented flagstones at Barnsley Gardens in Adairsville, Georgia. The stone wall is decorated with globular specimens of dwarf arborvitae (Thuja occidentalis 'Hetz Midget') planted above it.

held together by headers, making a very stable wall.

Save your very choicest flat rocks for the top course, as you'll find that people will use the wall to sit on and walk on. Again, these flat stones, called capstones, should cover joints between two rocks below them, and every 3 feet (1 m) one capstone should be large enough to cover the whole width of the wall from face to face (in a freestanding wall) or from face to bank.

Rainwater can pool in a dry wall, and then when it freezes, expand and push the stones around. A properly built wall, however, should not have such a problem. When a wall has the right batter and large capstones, rain won't easily penetrate it.

The gravel-filled spaces in the foundation stones, the inverted spine, the batter, and the capstones all contribute to preventing frost heaves. Whatever heaving occurs will be absorbed by the foundation spaces and the inverted spine as it moves upward and then settles back down.

If the wall will be much higher than 3 feet, consider extending a flat terrace of soil from it when you reach 4 feet (1.2 m), and building another wall of similar size at the back of the terrace. Work your way up the bank that way. You can build higher dry walls, but 3 to 4 feet seems an ideal size.

Plantings

Dry retaining walls provide a great opportunity for plantings—both those plants that grow or fall down over the face of the wall from the top, and those actually placed into soil packed into occasional channels that run from the face back to the bank. As you build your dry wall, here and there leave a slight space between two stones, and the ones behind them. Fill this space with soil that runs right back to the bank of soil behind the wall, and continue building courses on top of the channel. When the wall is finished, plant alyssum or other drought-tolerant plants in the exposed soil at the face. You'll find that a dry wall full of flowering alyssum in spring is a golden treat for the eyes.

Where the site is partially or fully shaded and moist, mosses may grow on the stones. This is devoutly to be wished, as emerald mosses look beautiful on stone walls. You can hasten this process by gathering mosses from stones in the woods and allowing them to dry out. When they are dry, crumble them into a fine powder and mix the powder with finely ground cornmeal. Use water to turn this mixture into a slurry and, using a wide paperhanger's brush, slop the mixture onto the bare rock surface of your newly laid wall. Moss spores in the slurry will grab onto the rock, and the cornmeal flour will provide some nourishment for them to get going. If you hit a dry spell, mist with the hose every day or two for a couple of weeks.

In sunny spots you may find stones with lichens already growing on them. Try to use these nicely patinated stones in the face of the wall where the lichens can be seen. They add color variation and texture to plain stone.

English ivy (Hedera helix) *is grown up this plain-board fence to form living bunting and wall sconces with Johnny-jump-ups* (Viola tricolor) *fill the spaces above the ivy.*

PROJECT ELEVEN

Paneled Wood Fence

(see page 66)

Construction is simple. Set the uprights at least 2 feet (.6 m) into a hole in which a large stone has been placed as a base for the post. Pour 6 inches (15 cm) of gravel, for drainage, into the hole and tamp it, then pour fresh concrete into the hole for another 4 inches to 6 inches. Stones and soil are tamped hard into the remaining space so that there's a berm of soil above the surrounding ground level. Alternatively, you can bring the concrete up to ground level, or forgo the concrete altogether and tamp stones and earth hard from the base stone to ground level and a little above.

Set these uprights at 8-foot (2.4 m) intervals so you can toenail 2-by-4s into them, or better, set the 2-by-4s into joist hangers that are nailed into the posts. Even better, dado the posts; that is, chisel out slots for the 2-by-4 rails to sit in, then nail them home.

The bottom rail should be set about 12 inches (31 cm) above the ground and the second one set along the top of the fence or very close to it. If the fence is going to be 6 feet (2 m) high or higher, place a third 2-by-4 about two-thirds of the way from the ground to the top of the fence. Make sure these rails are placed so that their widest side forms the vertical face.

Nail the boards to the rails using gal-vanized nails so they don't rust and discolor the boards. Use a level to make sure the boards are going on plumb, otherwise they'll make people woozy just looking at them. And don't bring the bottom of the boards down to ground level, but have them begin about 4 inches (10 cm) above ground level. Doing this prevents the bottom of the boards from sitting against the soil, soaking up moisture, and rotting.

PROJECT TWELVE

Wattle (see page 66)

A section of a wattle fence, called a hurdle, is woven through uprights that are set into a form on the ground, which is called a mold. To make a mold, use a heavy plank or heavy split log about 8 feet (2.4 m) long that is drilled with 1-inch (2.5 cm) holes every 10 inches (25 cm).

The uprights upon which the wattle will be woven, called sails, are stripped saplings cut where their bases are an inch in diameter so they fit snugly into the holes in the mold. Make sure they fit snugly and are straight, or the whole section will be skewed. Use good hardwood saplings of maple, hickory, black locust, ash, oak, or other durable wood. Trim off any branches as you peel the saplings.

The weaving material needs to be very flexible. Use hazel, hawthorn, willow, or any other slender, flexible, branchless whips. If you find a stand of brush whose

An English wattle hurdle provides an old-fashioned touch. Pliable saplings of alder or osier are woven through the uprights; young alder is planted in front of the fence and will overtake the hurdle within a few years, making a living fence.

young twigs seem to have the desired degree of flexibility, cut them off at ground level in winter, and they will send up straight, branchless whips in the spring. Gather them in spring and early summer when they are greenest and most flexible.

Starting at the bottom of the hurdle, a few inches above the ground, and using the thickest weaving rods there, tie one end of the first weaver to an end sail and begin to weave the rest of it through the sails, over and under alternate ones. When you reach the last sail, twist the weaver a half turn as you bring it around to begin weaving it on the way back. This is important, for if you don't twist them, the weavers will crack and break at these turns when they dry out, and the whole hurdle will lose its strength.

Using a billet, smack the woven rods down tightly against one another as you work them around the sails. In times gone by, the maker would leave a hole near the top, called a twilly hole, through which a rod could be inserted to lift the hurdle off the mold and carry it from place to place.

When you've woven all the way to the top, lift the sails and woven wattle off the mold. Cut the ends of the sails that were in the mold holes so they end in a point, and then drive these sails into the ground where you wish to set up your fence section.

PROJECT THIRTEEN

Picket Fence (see page 67)

To construct a picket fence, first figure roughly how many pickets you'll need. Determine how long the fence will be, and multiply the number by two, then add an extra quarter of that figure. For instance, if you plan a 200-foot (80 m) fence (an elaborate undertaking), figure 500 pickets.

Cut your 1-by-3s into 3-foot (1 m) or 4-foot (1.2 m) lengths, depending on how high you want the fence to be. Clamp four or five of these lengths together, and cut the points with a saber saw. For accuracy, you can make a pointed template from a piece of 1-by-3, lay it on the top picket so the point just touches the leading edge, and copy the point onto the picket with a pencil.

Calculate the length of the 4-by-4 posts as follows: If the pickets are 3 feet (1 m) tall, and you leave 2 inches (5 cm) between the bottom of the pickets and ground level, and if 2 feet (.6 m) of the posts are in the ground, you'll need your posts to be just shy of 6 feet (1.8 m), without finials. If your fence is to be 4 feet tall (1.2 m), the posts will have to be just shy of 7 feet (2.1 m).

Set dadoed 4-by-4 posts every 6 feet (1.8 m) and use 2-by-4s as rails. The bottom rail should run about 12 inches (31 cm) off the ground, and the top rail should be about 6 inches (15 cm) lower than the top of the 4-by-4. Discount any wooden balls, pineapples, or other lathed finials and

The orange blossoms of Lilium *'Enchantment' are enhanced by bee balm* (Monarda didyma), Lysimachia, *and solidago on this traditional white picket fence at Mrs. Rabion's garden in Milwaukee, Wisconsin.*

measure 6 inches below the place where the wood squares off into a 4-by-4. Make sure that your posts are plumb vertical and your rails dead level. The space between pickets should be less than the width of a picket—say, 2½ inches (6.3 cm). Create a spacer by making a piece of wood 2½ inches wide and somewhat longer than a picket. Using five screws so the block won't move, screw a block of wood onto the spacer near one end so that the block is true and square with the edges of the spacer. Using galvanized nails, nail on the first picket, making sure it is perfectly vertical. If the first one is off, the rest will be, too. The point of the picket should be level with the top of the 4-by-4, discounting any finials—that is, with the place where the post wood squares up.

After the first picket is nailed in place, put the spacer up snug against it, with the block of wood resting on the top rail, hold up the next picket, and nail it, then move the spacer, and continue. Check the verticality of your pickets every third one to make sure they are plumb. Then sight down the tops of the pickets and make sure that the points are all at the same level. You might stretch a taut, level line between posts to ensure the points are all at the same level. Don't let the line have any sag.

You can give a 4-foot (1.2 m) picket fence a swag by cutting 14 pairs of pickets, each pair shorter by ¾ inch (1.9 cm). Line up the pickets from the bottom as you nail them, and they will decrease toward the middle of a three-post run then increase again toward the next post. This arrangement looks best if the middle post, where

A simple stucco wall is set off by an ornate garden gate painted a rich sienna and crafted with two different kinds of lathe-turned balustrades, inset paneling, and black, wrought iron latches and angle braces.

the swag is at its bottom, is cut down to the height of the picket, rather than allowed to jut up. If one of the 14 pairs is cut at the regular length of 4 feet and the others shorter, the swag will run just 12 feet (3.6 m), or over three posts.

You can cut points, or cut the picket tops at a single angle, which was a common way to make a picket fence in colonial days. Or try any of a number of variations, such as rounded tops, varied-width pickets, or double-pointed tops. I'd stay away from picket slats cut straight across, which look like cheap snow fencing.

Once the fence is finished, give it a good coat of outdoor white paint. If you paint a picket fence any other color, you will probably wish it were white.

PROJECT FOURTEEN

Installing a Wooden Gate (see page 70)

If you are building a square wooden gate for your fence, take care not to install the gate's brace backward, a common mistake by amateur gate builders. Looking at the gate directly in front of you, let's say the hinges are on the left side of the square. The brace should then run from the lower left corner to the top right corner, running up and away from the bottom hinge. If the hinges are on the right as you look at the gate, the brace then runs from lower right to upper left.

For added strength, make rabbeted joints at the corners, rather than overlapping them. Fix the rabbeted joints together with wood screws. Then nail in the brace. You can then nail pickets or other decorative wood to the top and bottom rails, starting at the hinge side and making sure the picket doesn't interfere with the hinges. Now attach the hinges to the gate. Set the gate in place and prop it up on blocks so it's plumb. Mark the holes where the hinges will attach to the gatepost, remove the gate, predrill the holes, set the gate back in position, and fix it to the gatepost with screws. Remove the blocks and nail a stop on the side where the gate swings so it doesn't go past the opening and damage the hinges. Attach a latch. Choose one from the hardware store—there are many types. Thumb latches are the most common.

Incorporating Arches into a Gateway (see pages 70–72)

If the arch is for a gate through an existing fence, two of the arch's supporting posts can be attached to the fence, making the arch a functional pilaster. The two posts or legs out from the fence need to be securely anchored. A simple way to do this is to sink a 2-foot (.6 m) section of ceramic pipe, just slightly bigger around than the posts, into the ground, so that only an inch or two appears above ground. Pour in 6 inches (15 cm) of gravel, then some larger stones until the posts sit where they make the archway level. Finally, fill the pipe with wet cement to its top.

Another method is to make and bury a standard concrete footer with a 4-by-4 wooden center to a depth where the arch post sits on the 4-by-4 and the arch is level and plumb. Then attach a metal bracket to the 4-by-4, insert the posts into the bracket, and screw them in tightly. Trying to toenail the posts onto the 4-by-4 might result in split wood and a damaged archway, so it's best to avoid such jerrybuilding.

If there's no way to secure the archway to the fence, make footers or use pipes for all four arch posts. Sturdiness is not to be compromised unless you want to see the arch lying on its side some bright morning after a thunderstorm's furious winds have gusted the night before.

Cement hidden beneath this sinuous pebbled path ensures that the ferns, azaleas, and mondo grass (Ophiopogon japonicus) will not be able to invade the walkway.

Concrete and Pebble Path (see page 76)

The concrete needs to be poured into forms sunk into the soil where the path is to run. The concrete should be poured in 8-foot (2.4 m) sections with ½ inch (1.3 cm) of space between the sections, to act as expansion joints. The path can be as wide as you like, but as a general rule, no less than 4 feet (1.2 m) wide. In most gardens, there's no reason to make the path more than 6 or 7 feet wide.

When the concrete is wet, spread the pebbles evenly over the surface and press them down into the concrete with a float. Don't bury them—they should be just under the wet surface. When the concrete stiffens but before it sets completely hard, take a stiff-bristled push broom and a hose and alternately brush and hose the surface until the tops of the pebbles are exposed. Let the concrete set up hard, go over the surface with the broom a final time, then hose off the surface.

If you choose to use larger cobbles, you can use the same procedure as for the pebbles—sinking them in wet concrete— but make sure that you don't fill the form all the way to the top or concrete will spill out when you set in the stones. The cobbles need to be set with their flattest faces up, and buried at least two-thirds of the way into the concrete, otherwise the footing will be wobbly as visitors walk on the cobbles.

Another way to set larger cobbles into a walkway is to lay slabs of concrete underpinnings and then set the cobbles in mortar (one-third cement and two-thirds sand). Work in small sections, mixing mortar as you go. If you try to cover a slab with wet mortar and then set in cobbles, the mortar will harden before you get through the job. Mortar hardens past the point of workability in about two hours, so don't mix more mortar than you can use in that time.

Mortar each cobble in place. Again, flat sides give better footing. Make a pattern of stones in the section you're working on. When you start a new section with fresh mortar, slice away the dry surface of the previous section to expose still-moist mortar and spread fresh mortar onto that. Doing this will insure a good bond between the sections. With each new section, try a new idea for your stone pattern. This gives variety to the finished pathway.

Keep the stones you're working with in a pail of water so that they're thoroughly wet as you set them in place. Dry stones may bond poorly with the mortar because they will suck some of the moisture from the mortar and weaken it.

There's another way to do this: Build several forms about 2½ inches (6.4 cm) deep and set them on very smooth, flat ground, or nail a piece of plywood on the bottom. Keep each form to a size you'll be able to manage with a helper when it is filled with stones and concrete. Fill each form with one layer of stones with their flat sides down. Sweep enough sand over them so that about ½ inch (1.3 cm) filters down between the stones. Now pour concrete to fill the form. When the concrete is thoroughly dry, get some help, turn it over, and remove the wooden forms. Then move the slab to the place where you're building the walkway (obviously, it's a good idea to place the form right beside the walkway-in-progress). Dig a space large enough to accommodate each slab and place an inch of sand in the bottom. When the slab is in place, sweep out loose sand from between the stones, or wash it out with the hard jet from a hose.

If the pathway narrows or approaches steps, people may need to glance down to make sure of their footing. That's where you can do some stonework that will impress them. Use a variety of stones in differing sizes and colors at those places. Set some on edge, but buried deep in the mortar or cement so only their sides show. These can be arranged to flow along the ground like a school of fish, swimming side by side upstream.

PROJECT SEVENTEEN

Cement or Concrete Steps *(see pages 90–95)*

When making standard steps of concrete, you must first build a form for the risers and sides from wooden planks and excavate the soil behind the riser form. To insure stability, drive two or three lengths of metal pipe into the soil at least a foot (.3 m) deep, with about an inch less pipe protruding above the soil than the height of the riser.

Cement steps masquerade as stone in Harland Hand's garden in El Cerrito, California.

That way, the concrete will cover the pipe. You can use less concrete and maintain integrity by putting a few stones behind the riser form around the pipe.

Now fill the step with concrete and float the top of the concrete smooth. When it just begins to harden, but before it becomes stiff, pat the top with the float to pull up some nap on the concrete, or brush it with a steel brush, to give the step some roughness. Or use the technique described earlier for making a surface of pebbles. Just don't use stones that will make the step slick when it rains.

You can leave planting spaces in concrete steps by setting number 10 cans (1–1.5 l) on the soil at the side of a step and then pouring the concrete. When the concrete has hardened enough to hold its shape, twist and wiggle the can so it's free and then lift it out of the hole. When the concrete has finished hardening, fill the hole with good soil and put in your plants. Annuals are a good idea as they bloom over a long period of time, and you can pull out finished annuals and replace them with ones that will bloom through the remainder of the growing season until frost. You may choose to put in a perennial with pretty foliage, or use the hole as a receptacle for a potted plant that you can remove and replace when it's finished blooming.

Where importing or buying stones is not practical, it's also possible to make freestanding stepping "stones" of concrete or cement. Make mounds of concrete or cement when it's firm enough to hold its shape right in place where the steps are to go. Scuff their surfaces with a steel brush.

You can add some dry pigment such as a little brown or ocher to the cement when it is wet and freshly made if you want a natural color. After the wet cement is formed into a step, you can sprinkle its top with dry sand or a mixture of dry sand and cement to roughen it.

Flat Bridge (see page 96)

At both ends of the flat bridge, you'll need to build some kind of sturdy pier. Stones can be placed in a shallow excavation and fit together snugly to have a flat top on which a section of railroad tie is laid. The tie should extend beyond the ends of the stone underpinning. As you did with steps, you can drive a length of metal pipe through holes in the ends of the railroad tie sections and into the ground next to the stone underpinning.

The wood that spans the water should be sturdy—4-by-12 or 6-by-6 lengths of rot-resistant lumber are good. When rot-resistant 2-by-4s are nailed or screwed to the spans, their top surface should be just at the level of the path leading to the bridge, so that there's no rise or slight step to make people stumble. If there must be a step, make sure it's a noticeable one with a good 6-inch (15 cm) riser up to the surface of the bridge. Leave ¼ inch (.6 cm) of open space between the 2-by-4s so that rainwater and detritus can wash down and away.

Stepping Stones Across Slow Moving Water

(see pages 96–97)

To actually place the stepping stones, put on a pair of water shoes or rubber boots with steel-tipped toes (in case you drop a rock). Smooth the place where you want to put a stepping stone by clearing away any stones and leaving only washed gravel. Place the stone so that its flat-topped surface is about 3 to 4 inches (8–10 cm) above the surface of the water or mud. Use stones of similar size and place them so they protrude to the same height as your first rock. The flat surface on which people will step should be big enough to accommodate two full-sized adult feet placed side by side, even if only one foot will usually fall there.

If the stone wobbles at all, work with it until it's absolutely secure and stable. You may notice that no matter how you work a stone, you can't get it to grab a firm footing. In this case, you can make a form slightly larger than the stone, put in some fresh concrete, then the stone, and pour in more concrete so more than half the stone is covered, but plenty protrudes above the concrete so that all you will see above water is stone. When the concrete has set and is cured (about 3 days minimum), take off the form and set the flat concrete bottom snugly on the cleared creekbed. This process should give you a stable stone.

Before choosing stone to use, wet the stones and scuffle your foot on them. If they become slick or slippery when wet, find gritty or textured stones such as raw granite or sandstone that will give your feet good purchase.

In this Portland, Oregon, garden, the outflow from a slow-moving stream isn't carried under a bridge, but drains out between stones in a composite walkway. The stones are so wide and closely spaced that they offer the same protection from wet feet as a bridge would.

PROJECT TWENTY

Soft Landing for Play Equipment (see page 158)

To create a soft landing, excavate the area where a child will land to 18 inches (46 cm) deep. Edge the excavation all around but out of the landing area with planks nailed to stakes driven deep into the ground, so that the planks' top edges are flush with the ground level or just a quarter inch (6 mm) below it. Put a layer of coarse gravel 6 inches (15 cm) deep into the excavation, and cover this with porous ground cloth—the kind used as weed barriers that prevent weeds but allow rainwater to percolate through. Now add 12 inches (31 cm) of a soft material such as shredded bark or sand. (Cats may treat the thing as a giant litterbox; in this case, use shredded bark instead of sand.) Renew the bark or sand as necessary during the year. If a child lands hard, it's unlikely he'll have the wind knocked out of him.

PROJECT TWENTY-ONE

Tree House (see pages 159–61)

The main consideration with a tree house is that it should be safe. A square collar of 4-by-4s around the trunk of a generous,

In the Houston garden in Del Mar, California, a large specimen of Schinus terebinthifolius supports a treehouse that is at once exciting and safe.

sturdy tree can be supported by large posts set into concrete bases. Rather than dig holes for concrete right next to the tree trunk, which would involve cutting roots, build square boxes 2 feet (.6 m) on a side and 2 feet deep, place a flat stone in the bottom of each box and set a post upright on it, then fill the boxes with concrete. When the concrete sets, remove the concrete from the wooden boxes and set them around the tree so their posts support the square collar on top.

The collar then becomes a foundation for angled supports for the platform in the tree, avoiding the need for nailing wood to the tree. On the platform, build sides and

a roof if you want to make an actual all-weather tree house. Make sure the ladder is safe—a rope ladder is good exercise, it's safe, and the kids can pull it up so marauding pirates can't climb into their redoubt. Keep the platform, and thus the length of the ladder, to no more than 6 to 8 feet (1.8–2.4 m) above the ground, and install a soft safety surface where kids will land if they fall. Rises higher than 8 feet may require a check of local building codes and will become precarious indeed, unless secure and sturdy stairs with a handrail leading up to the house are constructed.

If the tree house is elaborate and heavy, make sure that the limbs on which it rests are strong, with wide crotches and no rot. Use additional supporting posts under the corners of the platform so that the entire load doesn't rest on the tree or the support collar mentioned above.

Sources

▣ Garden Sculpture, Pottery, and Artful Accoutrements

Architectural Pottery, 15161 Van Buren, Midway City, CA 92655 (714) 895-3359

Baker's Lawn Ornamentals, Somerset, PA (814) 445-7028

Cape Cod Cupola Co., Inc., 78 State Road, North Dartmouth, MA 02747 (508) 994-2119

Carruth Studio Inc., 1178 Farnsworth Road, Waterville, OH 43566 (800) 225-1178

Chestnut Knob, Box 4882, Martinsville, VA 24115 (800) 266-3035

Classic Garden Ornaments, Ltd., Longshadow Gardens, Pomona, IL 62975 (618) 893-4831

Claycraft, 807 Avenue of the Americas, New York, NY 10001 (212) 242-2903

Colonial Williamsburg Reproductions, P.O. Box 3532, Williamsburg, VA 23187 (800) 446-9240

Dennis Smith, 11055 Gambol Oak, Highland, UT 84003 (801) 756-6404

Design Toscano, 17 E. Campbell Street, Arlington Heights, IL 60005 (800) 525-1733

Devrou & Co. (topiary frames), P.O. Box 228, Jamestown, MI 49427 (616) 892-7544

Earthworks Co., P.O. Box 2396, Santa Barbara, CA 93105 (805) 963-4259

Florentine Craftsmen, Inc., 46-24 28th Street, Long Island City, NY 11101 (718) 937-7632

French Wyres, P.O. Box 131655, Tyler, TX 75713 (903) 597-8322

Garden Accents, 4 Union Hill Road, W. Conshohocken, PA 19428 (610) 825-5525

Garden Jazz (garden ornaments), (800) 511-0001

Gardener's Eden/Williams-Sonoma, 3250 Van Ness Avenue, San Francisco, CA 94109 (415) 421-7900

Gardener's Select, 110 West Elm Street, Tipp City, OH 45371 (800) 582-8527

Gardener's Supply Co., Burlington, VT (802) 863-1700

Gary Price Studio, 935 South 1000 East, Springville, UT 84663 (801) 489-6852

Haddonstone Ltd. (USA), 201 Heller Place, Bellmawr, NJ 08031 (609) 931-7011

Hen-Feathers & Co., Inc., 10 Balligomingo Road, Gulph Mills, PA 19428 (610) 277-0800

Irving & Jones, Inc., Village Center, Colebrook, CT 06021 (203) 379-9219

K. B. Maltz Sculpture Studio, P.O. Box 1867, Shelton, WA 98584 (360) 898-8822

Kenneth Lynch & Sons, 84 Danbury Road, Wilton, CT 06897 (203) 762-8363

Kinsman Company, River Road, Point Pleasant, PA 18950 (800) 733-4146

Langenbach (garden accoutrements catalog), P.O. Box 1420, Lawndale, CA 90260

Lumbini, San Francisco, CA (415) 863-5800

Maple Collections (800) 571-7609

McKinnon and Harris, P.O. Box 4885, Richmond, VA 23220 (804) 358-2385

Milaeger's Gardens, North Lima, OH (800) 669-9956

Mrs. McGregor's Garden Shop, Arlington, VA (703) 528-8773

New England Garden Ornaments, 38 E. Brookfield Road, North Brookfield, MA 01535 (508) 867-4474

Park Place, 2251 Wisconsin Avenue, NW, Washington, DC 20007 (202) 342-6294

Pompeian Studios, 90 Rockledge Road, Bronxville, NY 10708 (800) 457-5595

The Potted Plant, Atlanta, GA (404) 377-1494

Red Baron's, 6450 Roswell Road, Atlanta, GA 30328 (404) 252-3770

The Ryan Gainey Collection, 2973 Hardman Court, Atlanta, GA 30305 (404) 233-1805

Sculpture Placement Ltd., P.O. Box 9709, Washington, DC 20016 (202) 362-9310

Seibert & Rice, P.O. Box 365, Short Hills, NJ 07078 (201) 467-8266

Smith & Hawken, 117 East Strawberry Drive, Mill Valley, CA 94941 (415) 383-4415

Stone Forest, Box 2840, Santa Fe, NM 87504 (505) 986-8883

Tom Torrens Sculpture Design, Gig Harbor, WA (206) 857-5831

Vermont Garden Stone, 57 Pearl Street, Brandon, VT 05733 (802) 247-3653

The Well-Furnished Garden, Bethesda, MD (301) 469-6879

Wind & Weather, Mendocino, CA (800) 922-9463

Winterthur Reproductions, P.O. Box LNR, Winterthur, DE 19735 (800) 448-3883

◙ Garden Structures

Amdega Machin Conservatories, P.O. Box 7, Glenview, IL 60025 (800) 922-0110

Anderson Design Arbors and Trellises, P.O. Box 4057, Bellingham, WA 98227 (800) 947-7697

Bamboo Fencer, 31 Germania Street, Jamaica Plain, Boston, MA 02130 (617) 524-6137

BowBends Bell Top Gazebos, Box 900, Bolton, MA 01740

City Visions, Inc., 311 Seymour Street, Lansing, MI 48933 (517) 372-3385

Country Casual, 17317 Germantown Road, Suite 4156, Germantown, MD 20874 (301) 540-0040

Dalton Pavilions, Inc., 20 Commerce Drive, Telford, PA 18969 (215) 721-1492

Gardener's Supply Co., Burlington, VT (802) 863-1700

Gardensheds, 651 Millcross Road, Lancaster, PA 17601 (717) 397-5430

Garden Trellises, Box 105, LaFayette, NY 13084 (315) 498-9003

Janco Greenhouses, 9390 Davis Avenue, Laurel, MD 20723 (800) 323-6933

New England Garden Ornaments, 38 E. Brookfield Road, North Brookfield, MA 01535 (508) 867-4474

Oak Leaf Conservatories of York, 876 Davis Drive, Atlanta, GA 30327 (800) 360-6283

Plow & Hearth, P.O. Box 5000, Madison, VA 22727 (800) 627-1712

Private Garden, 10 Allen Street, Hampden, MA 01036 (413) 566-0277

Sturdi-Built Greenhouse Mfg. Co., 11304 SW Boones Ferry Road, Portland, OR 97219 (800) 722-4115

Sunspot Inc., 5030 40th Avenue, Hudsonville, MI 49426 (800) 635-4786

Trellis Structures, Box 380, Beverly, MA 01915 (978) 921-1235

Under Glass Mfg. Corp., P.O. Box 798, Lake Katrine, NY 12449 (914) 336-5050

The Valencia Garden Buildings, 2673 87th Street SW, 4th Floor, Byron Center, MI 49315 (616) 878-4200

Vixen Hill Gazebos, Main Street, Elverson, PA 19520 (800) 423-2766

Walpole Woodworkers, 767 East Street, Walpole, MA 02081 (800) 343-6948

Wintergarden Conservatories, 5153 North Clark Street, Suite 228, Chicago, IL 60640 (773) 506-8000

◙ Garden Furniture

Adirondack Designs, 350 Cypress Street, Fort Bragg, CA 95437 (800) 222-0343

Barlow Tyrie Inc., 1263 Glen Avenue, Suite 230, Moorestown, NJ 08057 (609) 273-7878

The Bench Smith, P.O. Box 86, Warrington, PA 18976 (800) 482-3327

Brown Jordan, 9860 Gidley Street, El Monte, CA 91731 (626) 443-8971

Chaise de Soleil, Palm Beach, FL/Lagunitas, CA (800) 354-3511

Eden's Gate, 38 Barnard Street, Savannah, GA 31401 (912) 234-8323

McGuire, 151 Vermont Street, San Francisco, CA 94103 (415) 986-0812

Park Place, 2251 Wisconsin Avenue, NW, Washington, DC 20007 (202) 342-6294

Plow & Hearth, P.O. Box 5000, Madison, VA 22727 (800) 627-1712

Reed Brothers Carved Furniture, 5000 Turner Road, Sebastopol, CA 95472 (707) 795-6261

Tidewater Workshop, Oceanville, NJ 08231 (800) 666-8433

Weatherend Estate Furniture, Rockland, ME (800) 456-6483

Wood Classics, Box 97, Gardiner, NY (914) 255-5651

◙ Building and Paving Materials

Paris Ceramics, 150 E. 58th Street, 7th Floor, New York, NY 10155 (212) 644-2782

◙ Outdoor Lighting

Classic & Country Crafts, 5100-1B Clayton Road, Suite 291, Concord, CA 94521 (510) 672-4337

Comtrad Industries, 2820 Waterford Lake Drive, Suite 102, Midlothian, VA 23113 (800) 992-2966

Doner Design Inc., 2175 Beaver Valley Pike, New Providence, PA 17560 (717) 786-8891

Escort Lighting, 201 Sweitzer Road, Sinking Spring, PA 19608 (800) 856-7948

Liteform Designs, P.O. Box 3316, Portland, OR 97208 (503) 257-8464

◙ Water Gardening Equipment

Lilypons Water Gardens, P.O. Box 10, Buckeystown, MD 21717 (800) 723-7667

Paradise Water Gardens, 80 May Street, Whitman, MA 02382 (800) 955-0161

Perry's Water Gardens, 1831 Leatherman Gap Road, Franklin, NC 28734 (704) 524-3264

Resource Conservation Technology, Inc. (pond liners), 2633 North Calvert Street, Baltimore, MD 21218 (800) 477-7724

Tetra Pond, 3001 Commerce Street, Blacksburg, VA 24060 (540) 951-5400

Waterford Gardens, 74 East Allendale Road, Saddle River, NJ 07458 (201) 327-0721

William Tricker, Inc., 7125 Tanglewood Drive, Independence, OH 44131 (800) 524-3492

◙ Bird Supplies

B&B Nurseries, P.O. Box 1057, Morrisville, VT 05661 (800) 724-7284

Duncraft Bird Supplies, Penacook, NH 03303-9020 (800) 763-7878

Index

For Elizabeth and Allison
— Jeff Cox

In addition to all the gardens, gardeners, and garden designers
mentioned in the captions, I would like to give thanks to Jan Rose
and Trish Bryant. Without their help, this project and most of
the others that we work on together would not be possible. And
special thanks to Susan Costello at Abbeville Press for giving me
the encouragement and the time to express my thoughts in images
and then doing such a terrific job in pulling it all together.
— Jerry Pavia

Front cover: A comfortable garden seat beneath a fiery explosion of
    bougainvillea in Jane Paulson's garden, Santa Barbara, California.
Back cover: A rustic two-story bird feeder in Jody Honnen's garden
    in Rancho Santa Fe, California.
Frontispiece: Welcoming curves of the pathway and gate at Jody
    Honnen's garden.
Page 4: A birdbath and a variety of herbs in Sarah Hammond's garden
    in Bolinas, California.
Page 5 (clockwise from top right): the Steele family garden in Richmond,
    Virginia; the Wallace family garden in Santa Barbara, California; the
    Steele family garden in Richmond, Virginia; Sally Cooper's garden
    in Charlotte, North Carolina; Jeanne Lipsitt's garden in Norcross,
    Georgia; Hellie Robertson's garden in San Anselmo, California; the
    Jim Gibbs garden in Ball Ground, Georgia; a garden in Lake Oswego,
    Oregon; the Moss family garden in Saugus, California; the Roberts
    family garden in Friday Harbor, Washington.

Editor: Susan Costello
Production Editor: Abigail Asher
Designer: Molly Shields
Layout: Barbara Balch
Production Director: Hope Koturo

Text copyright © 1999 Jeff Cox. Photographs copyright © 1999 Jerry
Pavia. Compilation, including selection and placement of text and
images, copyright © 1999 Abbeville Press. All rights reserved under
international copyright conventions. No part of this book may be
reproduced or utilized in any form or by any means, electronic or
mechanical, including photocopying, recording, or by any information
storage and retrieval system, without permission in writing from the
publisher. Inquiries should be addressed to Abbeville Publishing
Group, 22 Cortlandt Street, New York, N.Y. 10007. The text of this
book was set in Meta Plus and Electra.
Printed and bound in China.

First edition
10 9 8 7 6 5 4 3 2 1

Library of Congress Cataloging-in-Publication Data
Cox, Jeff, 1940–
    Decorating your garden / text by Jeff Cox ; photographs
by Jerry Pavia
        p.   cm.
    Includes index.
    ISBN 0-7892-0229-8
    1. Garden ornaments and furniture.   2. Garden structures.
I. Title.
SB473.5.C69   1999
717—dc21   98-40477